# laügh

## your way

## through

## grammar

# Joan D. Berbrich, Ph.D.

**Amsco books by Joan D. Berbrich**

Fifteen Steps to Better Writing
Laugh Your Way Through Grammar
Macbeth: A Resource Book
101 Ways to Learn Vocabulary
Reading Around the World
Reading Today
Thirteen Steps to Better Writing
Wide World of Words
Writing About Amusing Things
Writing About Curious Things
Writing About Fascinating Things
Writing About People
Writing Creatively
Writing Logically
Writing Practically

# laügh
## your way
## through
## grammar

*Dedicated to serving*

**AMSCO**

*our nation's youth*

**Amsco School Publications, Inc.**
315 Hudson Street/New York, N.Y. 10013

When ordering this book, please specify:
either **R 498 BS** or
LAUGH YOUR WAY THROUGH GRAMMAR
BLUE TEXT, SOFTBOUND

ISBN 0-87720-785-2

Printed in the United States of America

# To the Student

The English language is fascinating!

*A single word can make a difference . . .*

Would you rather have your teacher say . . . ?

**There are few errors in your essay.**

or

**There are a few errors in your essay.**

*Even a single space can make a difference . . .*

Which would please your mother more?

**You are a grandmother.**

or

**You are a grand mother.**

*A confused word can make a difference . . .*

**No reading ALOUD in the library.**

**No reading ALLOWED in the library.**

Which sign would your librarian post?

*A comma instead of an apostrophe can make a difference . . .*

Newspaper ad:

**COME EARLY. WIDE SELECTION OF BOOKS, KIDS, [*sic*] TOYS, AND CLOTHING AVAILABLE!**

(And some people think selling kids is illegal!)

*And several punctuation marks can make a difference . . .*

Try reading this sentence:

**It was and I said not but.** (Can't do it? Try below.)
**"It was 'and'," I said, "not 'but'."**

v

The English language is fascinating. Because it is rich and varied and replete with nuances, you can do all sorts of things with it.

*You can fiddle with rhyme . . .*

If a healthy captain is a **chipper skipper,** what is a cautious scholar?

A **prudent student,** of course!

*You can enjoy a pun based on the two meanings of a word . . .*

What is the longest sentence in the world?

**Go to prison for life.**

*You can chuckle at the adverb antics that make a Tom Swiftie . . .*

**"My pencil needs sharpening," Tom said dully.**

*You can create a pun based on the two meanings of a letter . . .*

What letter is the target of a sailor's love?

**The letter "C" (sea).**

*You can develop a riddle based on words that are parts of other words . . .*

What kind of sense has no meaning?

**NONsense!**

*You can chuckle . . .*

at a sign in a deli:

**"Our TONGUE Speaks for Itself."**

at a kangaroo word:

**There is a BLOOM in BLOssOM, and a MALE in MAscuLinE.**

at a tongue-in-cheek quip:

**Old teachers never die; they just lose their class!**

vi

This wordplay, this ability to have verbal fun is possible only if you become truly familiar with our common language. Of course, wordplay is serious, too. You are playing with words every time you write a sentence. You choose particular words, and you choose to order them in a particular way. The result is your personal style (or—sadly—lack of style!).

This text is designed to make you more sensitive, more alert, more knowledgeable about serious wordplay (sometimes called grammar!) and—at the same time—to increase your skills with amusing wordplay: in other words, to help you have fun with words.

Many of the sentences used in the text proper (Sections II through V) and most of the sentences used in the Practice Sessions (Section I) are based on jokes, riddles, quips, or trivia items. They should appeal to your funny bone, hold your interest, and make grammar "user-friendly." (For those of you who are not hackers, the hyphenated expression is computer lingo!)

We hope this book will do what it is designed to do—to help you to a mastery of the English language as you chuckle—giggle—and LAUGH YOUR WAY THROUGH GRAMMAR!

# Instructions for the Practice Sessions

There is no easy road to good grammar . . . but there are roads that are interesting, challenging, and even—fun! Here's how to travel the particular road provided in this text.

1. Turn to Practice Session (PS) 1. Notice the title: "Mixed Bag." This title tells you that you can expect to find *any* type of error in this PS: grammar, usage, punctuation, capitalization, even spelling. PS 2, on the other hand, bears the title: "Sentence Structure." This title tells you that the errors in this PS are limited to sentence structure errors.

2. Read the directions given directly under the title. Directions will vary from PS to PS, so it is important that you understand what you are expected to do.

3. Now you are ready for the first problem. Read sentence #1. Can you spot the error? Remember—since this PS is a "Mixed Bag," you will have to be alert for all types of errors. If you find the error quickly, good for you! If you don't (or if you want to check your answer), look at the reference number (in parentheses) which follows the sentence. In this case the number is 10-b.

4. Next turn to the text proper (Sections II–V). Look for #10 (page 66). When you find it, you will discover that #10 covers the four types of sentences. Check part "b." It tells you what an interrogative sentence is and how to punctuate one. Now—looking back at the first sentence in PS 1, you will see that "What did Adam eat before Eve was created" is, of course, an interrogative sentence and must be followed by a question mark. All clear?

5. Follow this same procedure with the rest of the sentences in PS 1. If you own this book, you may place a check mark to the left of any sentence you were unable to correct. **If you do not own this book, do not write in it.** Instead, enter the error in your notebook. You should quickly learn your strong and weak points: the rules you know and the rules you don't know. And this, in turn, will help you to concentrate on your own grammatical idiosyncrasies.

*Summary:* Please notice that you are *not* being asked to learn great blocks of grammar. You are *not* being asked to memorize 500 rules. You are *not* being asked to wade through exercises of ten, or twenty, or thirty sentences with the same type of error until you nod with boredom. Instead, you are being asked to be your own physician: to diagnose, to understand, and to correct. While you enjoy the content of the sentences in the Practice Sessions, you will discover your own grammatical weaknesses and will learn how to overcome them.

We hope you will do each Practice Session not once but many times. First work with each PS thoroughly. Then, as you browse a second, a third, or a tenth time through familiar jokes and fascinating facts, continue the procedure, detecting errors, correcting them, checking them in the text proper. You will learn easily and painlessly (at least we hope you will), and the result should be better speech, better writing, and a more sophisticated sense of humor.

ENJOY . . . .

---

If your teacher insists that the English language is easy, refer her or him to this bit of doggerel. (The author's name seems to have disappeared.)

> One fowl is a goose, but two are called geese,
> Yet the plural of mouse should never be meese.

> If I speak of a foot and you show me your feet,
> And I give you a boot, would a pair be called beet?

> If one is a tooth, and the whole set are teeth,
> Why should not the plural of booth be called beeth?

*Joan D. Berbrich*

# Contents

For a more detailed Table of Contents in any section,
turn to the first page of that section.

# SECTION I

# Practice Sessions

---

*Continued on Following Page*

1

## PRACTICE SESSION 1—Mixed Bag

Each sentence below contains an error. Find it; understand why it is wrong; know how to correct it.

1. What did Adam eat before Eve was created. Spare ribs, of course! **(10-b)**

2. A bus driver is a person who tells everyone where to get off at. **(101)**

3. When asked how he hit so many home runs, Babe Ruth said, I just keep swinging. **(225-a)**

4. Strawberry jam is found on bread children and piano keys. **(224-a)**

5. "I'm drowning" he shouted. **(10-d)**

6. The robber was described as a man six feet tall with a mustache weighing 170 pounds. **(15-c)**

7. Most parents being on speaking terms with God and spanking terms with their children. **(12-b)**

8. The person with push don't need pull. **(127)**

9. There ain't much fun in medicine, but there's a good deal of medicine in fun! **(84)**

10. It's been some day! I should have stood in bed! **(191)**

11. The computer doesn't eliminate red tape it only perforates it! **(13)**

12. My boss she comes in early to see who comes in late. **(37-b)**

13. Today most of the food are coming pre-packaged— including food for thought! **(29-c)**

14. Jake and him take their hats off to one man: their barber! **(33-b)**

15. Its easier to live within an income than without one! **(35-c)**

16. Swallow your pride occasionally, it's non-fattening! **(14)**

17. I always feel sad in the fall when the trees shed their leafs and the baseball clubs their managers! **(23-f)**

18. Fried dough, bread dough fried in deep fat, is also called "huffle-duffle" and "morning glory," but only the later term is used in my hometown. **(158)**

## PRACTICE SESSION 2—Sentence Structure

Each sentence below contains a sentence structure error. (Review #10, 11, 12, 13, 14.) Identify each error; understand it; correct it.

1. The boss told the new secretary she should have been at her desk at 9 o'clock she asked innocently: ''Why? What happened?'' **(13)**

2. If they had considered the pig and its potential as an acrobat and tight-rope walker. **(12-c)**

3. A flea can jump twelve inches, twelve inches for a flea is equal to two football fields for a person five feet tall. **(14)**

4. Parents of teenagers may well resent President James Garfield, in 1878, he was the first President to use a telephone! **(14)**

5. Suburbia is a place where a developer takes out all the trees then he names the streets Maple, Pine, and Elm! **(13)**

6. Went ice fishing and came home with fifty pounds of ice. **(12-a)**

7. One candy maker turns any portrait into a bas-relief replica made of chocolate, now you can eat yourself! **(14)**

8. A king is wise if he has several court jesters. Because then he'll always keep his wits about him! **(12-e)**

9. We're having sponge cake for dessert I sponged the eggs from Mrs. Jones and the milk from Mrs. Black! **(13)**

10. Jesse Lasky, the movie magnate, had three large hills removed from in front of his ranch house they were blocking his view! **(13)**

11. Ten-year-old Zach soon discovered he could make money with his bugle, his father paid him a dollar a week not to play it! **(14)**

12. A pumpkin with fifteen miles of roots not being unusual. **(12-b)**

13. Sarah Bernhardt, the great actress, liked to bathe in milk. Also to receive callers while she was in the bathtub. **(12-f)**

14. Six-year-old Jimmy attended church for the first time he liked the music but said the commercial was too long! **(13)**

15. If you're right-handed, the fingernails on your right hand grow faster, if you're left-handed, the reverse is true. **(14)**

*Laugh Your Way Through Grammar*

## PRACTICE SESSION 3—Mixed Bag

Each sentence below contains an error. Find it; understand it; correct it.

1. Shouldn't an autobiography be the life story of a *car*.  **(10-b)**

2. A bachelor's favorite dish is any dish that's all ready washed!  **(90)**

3. When he points a finger at someone, he's pointing three at hisself.  **(27)**

4. The ship sank with everyone aboard except one lady passenger. She was heavily insured and carried a cargo of pig iron.  **(36-h.1)**

5. With those kind of prices, money doesn't talk—it whimpers.  **(197)**

6. When an apple and a banana fight, the banana always runs away because it's real yellow!  **(63-d)**

7. Mike and me learned there's an island called "If" in the Mediterranean.  **(33-b)**

8. (short history of money) Here it is! They're it goes!  **(194)**

9. A billion seconds ago it was 1951, a billion minutes ago Jesus was alive, a billion hours ago our ancestors were living in the Stone Age.  **(14-c, 222-c)**

10. The world is moving so fast that whomever says something can't be done is generally interrupted by someone who is doing it!  **(30-d)**

11. He should of realized that a man who's wrapped up in himself makes a mighty small parcel!  **(119)**

12. The truth may hurt for awhile, but a lie is agony for a lifetime.  **(102)**

13. The children brung their pet hamsters to school.  **(41-b,d)**

14. Inside of a week, the florist learned that his daughter was a budding genius and his son a blooming idiot!  **(152)**

15. The principle part of a horse is its "mane"!  **(180)**

16. Some people don't lose anything accept their temper when they diet!  **(77)**

17. Sunday is the stronger day of the week because all the rest are "weak" days.  **(55-c)**

18. The favorite exercise for them women is hunting bargains!  **(37-d)**

## PRACTICE SESSION 4—Spelling

Which word in each set of parentheses is spelled correctly?

1. When a big-game hunter (disappears, dissappears), something he disagreed with ate him!   **(232-a)**

2. Silly Suzy washed ice cubes in hot water and then (cried, cryed) because she couldn't find them!   **(235-a)**

3. What happened to the kitten that fell into the photocopy machine in the (laboratory, labratory)? (Answer: it became a copycat.)   **(238)**

4. Next to the (calendar, calender) on the wall of the cafeteria was this sign: COURTEOUS AND EFFICIENT SELF-SERVICE.   **(237)**

5. She (paniced, panicked) when she heard that, in the theater, a poor house tonight may mean the poorhouse tomorrow.   **(236)**

6. The (February, Febuary) concert at the jail was a "cell" out!   **(238)**

7. Frankenstein was a lonely man (until, untill) he learned to *make* friends!   **(237)**

8. He (accidentally, accidently) ate his words and found them sharp.   **(233-a)**

9. Nothing is so (embarassing, embarrassing) as watching your boss do something you told him couldn't be done.   **(237)**

10. She (prefered, preferred) the stock market as an exercise place: she ran scared, lifted her hopes, and pushed her luck!   **(233-d)**

11. Try not to (mispell, misspell) any words in this sentence.   **(232-a)**

12. People who go in for (bookeeping, bookkeeping) end up paying library fines!   **(237)**

13. His (grammar, grammer) is as horrendous as his spelling!   **(238)**

14. A (peice, piece) of pie isn't fattening—not the way some restaurants now slice it!   **(234-b, 238)**

15. In 1910 in Waterloo, Nebraska, a law was passed making it (ilegal, illegal) for a barber to eat onions between 7 a.m. and 7 p.m.   **(232-a)**

16. It (occured, occurred) to me that a theater is a sad place because all the seats are in "tiers."   **(233-d)**

## PRACTICE SESSION 5—Noun Plurals and Apostrophes

(Review #23.) Preceding each sentence is a singular noun. What is its plural form?

1. **(radio)** Wicked Willie asked if the angels sing and play harps because they haven't any __?__ . **(23-d)**

2. **(sandwich)** Sign in deli: OUR TONGUE __?__ SPEAK FOR THEM-SELVES. **(23-a)**

3. **(turkey)** Wild __?__ not only can fly; they also can take off vertically. **(23-c)**

4. **(teaspoonful)** There are as many molecules in a teaspoonful of water as there are __?__ of water in the Atlantic Ocean. **(23-m)**

5. **(son-in-law)** "You make me jump for joy," the trampoline expert said to her two __?__ . **(23-l)**

6. **(ox)** Babe, Paul Bunyan's blue ox, was truly an ox above all other __?__ . **(23-g)**

7. **(baby)** Eight-year-old Jessie announced that she'd learned how to make __?__ . "All you do," she said triumphantly, "is drop the *y* and add *ies*." **(23-b)**

8. **(church)** All __?__ should post this sign: "This is a ch __ __ ch. What's missing?" (Answer: u r.) **(23-a)**

9. **(potato)** When do Irish __?__ change nationality? (Answer: when they are French fried.) **(23-e)**

(Review #24, 35, 226.) In each sentence find the error and know how to correct it.

10. A quarter isnt as good as a dollar, but it goes to church more often! **(226-a)**

11. Otto is Sgt. Snorkels dog in the comic strip "Beetle Bailey." **(24-a)**

12. "Nothing" may be defined as a balloon with it's skin off. **(35-c)**

13. The Secretary of States philosophy is that history repeats itself because most people weren't listening the first time! **(24-e)**

14. Rabbits ears are large because rabbits, almost defenseless, need to hear approaching danger. **(24-d)**

## PRACTICE SESSION 6—Mixed Bag

In each sentence find the error; understand it; correct it.

1. The meek shall inherit the earth, but how long will they stay meek after they get it. **(10-b)**

2. Chimnies, according to one wit, might well be called fire escapes! **(23-c)**

3. The five Bs of middle age are baldness, bridgework, bifocals, bay-windows, and bunions. **(225-b, 226-b)**

4. She surprised Al and I when she said that during the French Revolution some prisoners played with a yo-yo on the way to the guillotine. **(34-a,d)**

5. Margaret Whiting attended a boring Broadway premiere she noted, ''I've seen more excitement at the opening of an umbrella.'' **(13)**

6. The three alumnuses agreed that a synonym is a word you use when you can't spell the other word! **(23-o)**

7. The Murphies told us that plenty of houses are now being put up—in price! **(23-b)**

8. Our local baseball team is non-violent; they havent hit anything in weeks! **(226-a)**

9. A weather forecaster is someone with which the weather doesn't always agree. **(37-f.3, 203)**

10. Few things get kicked as much as the seat of goverment. **(233-a)**

11. Timid people are sheeps in sheep's clothing. **(23-i)**

12. What this country needs is the spirit of 76 and the prices of 36. **(226-a)**

13. The ''Gettysburg Address'' was written while traveling from Washington on the back of an envelope. **(15, 16)**

14. The passerbys chuckled when the street lecturer defined anxiety as what a Volkswagen driver feels when the car is surrounded by a pack of Dobermans! **(23-l)**

15. Us relatives call our rich uncle ''a kin we love to touch.'' **(37-c)**

16. The check you sent I recieved twice: once from you and once from the bank. **(234-c)**

## PRACTICE SESSION 7—Mixed Bag

Each sentence below contains an underlined expression. Below each sentence are four possible answers. Which one is correct?

1. A gigasecond is a billion <u>seconds, you</u> are past thirty-two before you've reached your first gigasecond! **(14)**

    a. Correct as is
    b. scconds; you
    c. seconds. you
    d. seconds you

2. The two jungle lions were whispering to <u>one another—"Let</u> us prey!" **(128, 209-a)**

    a. Correct as is
    b. each other—"Let
    c. one another—"let
    d. each other—"let

3. The penalty for bigamy is two <u>mother-in-laws.</u> **(23-l)**

    a. Correct as is
    b. mother-in-law's
    c. mothers-in-law
    d. mothers'-in-law

4. <u>Ann's and Jen's</u> new doctor doll operates on batteries. **(24-f)**

    a. Correct as is
    b. Ann and Jen's
    c. Anns' and Jens'
    d. Ann's and Jen

5. "Teenage boys will drive anything," my father told <u>Tim and I,</u> "except a lawnmower." **(34-d, 224-r)**

    a. Correct as is
    b. Tim and me,
    c. Tim and I;
    d. Tim and me;

6. Some of the hens <u>gets discouraged because</u> they never find things where they laid them! **(11-c.2, 29-c, 47-h)**

    a. Correct as is
    b. gets discouraged, because
    c. get discouraged because
    d. get discouraged, because

7. Motorized skateboards can travel at twenty miles per <u>hour; each</u> board has a small gas tank attached at the rear. **(11-b.2)**

    a. Correct as is
    b. hour: each
    c. hour, each
    d. hour. each

8. If everybody obeyed the <u>ten Commandments there</u> would be no eleven o'clock news. **(11-c.1, 214-c)**

    a. Correct as is
    b. Ten Commandments,
    c. ten Commandments;
    d. ten Commandments,

## PRACTICE SESSION 8—Case of Personal Pronouns

Which pronoun in each set of parentheses is correct? Why? (Review #26–27, 32–35.)

1. It was (her, she) who told me that middle age is the time your legs buckle and your belt doesn't!  **(33-d)**

2. Between you and (I, me), he's not as big a fool as he used to be—he's lost weight!  **(34-c)**

3. Our minds are made up—don't confuse my brothers and (I, me) with the facts!  **(34-a,d.1)**

4. In his spare time the novelist Balzac amused (himself, hisself) by drawing portraits with crayons.  **(27)**

5. He went to the drive-in bank to show his car to (its, it's) real owner!  **(35-c)**

6. Frank asked (her, she) and her sister this riddle: "What happens to liars when they die?" The girls replied: "They lie still!"  **(34-b,d.2)**

7. My mother and (me, myself, I) invented a solar-powered clothes dryer: it's called a clothesline!  **(33-b,e.1; 27-c)**

8. It fascinated my sister and (I, me) when we heard that one pig out of every twenty has an ulcer.  **(34-a,d.1)**

9. Could it have been (her, she) and her sister who wondered what Swiss cheese would taste like if it weren't ventilated?  **(33-c,d)**

10. I was amused by that last statement of (hers, her's)—that if you've read one dictionary, you've read them all!  **(35-b)**

11. Did Zach and (her, she) tell you that butterflies were once called "flutterbys"?  **(33-c, b)**

12. Those parents of (theirs, their's) named the twins Kate and Duplicate!  **(35-b)**

13. According to (he, him) and his sister, in Japan the children often teach mice to dance.  **(34-c,d.3)**

14. Celebrities are people who pat (theirselves, themselves) on the shoulder while giving the cold shoulder to noncelebrities!  **(27)**

## PRACTICE SESSION 9—Colon and Semicolon

In each sentence find the error; understand it; correct it. (Review #222, 223.)

1. A pun is a play on words, for example, a "male (mail) carrier" is the mother of a baby boy! **(222-b)**

2. I had lunch with John Travolta, the movie star, Baryshnikov, the ballet dancer, and Leontyne Price, the opera singer. **(222-c)**

3. She'd be a good dancer except for two things, her feet! **(223-b)**

4. Some people seem to think that these are the four most important words in English, I, me, mine, and money! **(223-a)**

5. Slice the top and the bottom off a rubber ball what's left was the first hockey puck. **(223-b)**

6. All through *Gone With the Wind*, Scarlett O'Hara repeats one statement "I'll think about it tomorrow." **(223-c)**

7. The hardest time to raise children is at 6.30 a.m.! **(223-e)**

8. Gerald Ford was once named Leslie King, hence a King became President of the United States! **(222-b)**

9. After shopping for three hours, she came home with a red, white, and blue dirndl, a large, expensive radio, a yellow, green, and orange bedspread, and a doll. **(222-c)**

10. Mike weighs himself 5,000 times a day, he has a job checking the accuracy of scales. **(222-a)**

11. The golf caddies of Sri Lanka use their toes to pick up golf balls they are too dignified to stoop! **(223-b)**

12. If you need a good doctor, contact: Dr. Frank Ellison, Dr. Pat King, or Dr. Helen Morgan. **(223-a)**

13. A loafer is someone who naps all day and wakes up at 4.30 p.m.—in order to go home! **(223-e)**

14. Heaven is a place of bliss, hell is a place of blisters. **(222-a)**

15. Winston Churchill took a nap every day Napoleon followed the same custom. **(222-a)**

16. Only one major sport started in this country, basketball. **(223-b)**

## PRACTICE SESSION 10—Punctuation Makes a Difference!

Is punctuation important? See for yourself! Can you explain clearly the difference between the two sentences in each of the following pairs?

1. SLOW—MEN AT WORK
   SLOW MEN AT WORK

2. We Sell Deer, Food, and Nuts
   We Sell Deer Food and Nuts

3. Woman without her man would be a savage.
   Woman—without her, man would be a savage.

4. The lawyer said the doctor is a fool.
   "The lawyer," said the doctor, "is a fool."

5. For Sale: Pony, saddle, and bridle, $45.
   For Sale: Pony saddle and bridle, $45.

6. Motel sign: We have no smoking rooms available.
   We have no-smoking rooms available.

7. I intend to serve fairly, honestly, and energetically.
   I intend to serve fairly honestly and energetically.

8. We bought a little-used car.
   We bought a little used car.

9. Mr. Madison, the butcher, is dishonest.
   Mr. Madison, the butcher is dishonest.

10. The magician dropped, a bullet in her mouth.
    The magician dropped a bullet in her mouth.

11. Let's eat, Ellie, and then go to the baseball game.
    Let's eat Ellie, and then go to the baseball game.

12. The actor, recently blasted by the critics, and his wife arrived in New York City yesterday.
    The actor, recently blasted by the critics and his wife, arrived in New York City yesterday.

13. Children—drive slow.
    Children, drive slow.

14. The snake killed, the scout, Tom Madigan, grinned.
    The snake killed the scout; Tom Madigan grinned.

*Laugh Your Way Through Grammar*

## PRACTICE SESSION 11—Mixed Bag

Each sentence below contains an underlined expression. Below each sentence are four possible answers. Which one is correct?

1. "The one who beat the drum and whipped the cream wasn't <u>me</u>", she protested.   **(33-d, 225-g)**

   *a.* Correct as is

   *b.* me," she

   *c.* I," she

   *d.* I", she

2. Don't be embarrassed by misspelling "embarrassment": remember there are two <u>"r's"</u> and two <u>"s's"</u>.   **(23-n, 220-c, 225-b)**

   *a.* Correct as is

   *b.* "rs" and "ss".

   *c.* r's and s's.

   *d.* "r's" and "s's."

3. A small knife is commonly called a <u>penknife. Since</u> it was originally used to sharpen goose quills to be used as pens.   **(12-e, 11-c.2)**

   *a.* Correct as is

   *b.* penknife; since

   *c.* penknife: since

   *d.* penknife since

4. A Yale student asked Harry Truman how to get started in politics. "You've <u>all ready started</u>," retorted the former President. "You're spending somebody else's money, aren't you?"   **(90, 225-g)**

   *a.* Correct as is

   *b.* all ready started",

   *c.* already started",

   *d.* already started,"

5. My <u>father-in-laws argument was sound</u>—more sound!   **(24-c, 237)**

   *a.* Correct as is

   *b.* father-in-law's argument

   *c.* father-in-law's arguement

   *d.* father's-in-law arguement

6. When the tramp asked for something <u>to eat the farmer</u> suggested he go to the woodshed and take a few chops!   **(11-c.1, 198)**

   *a.* Correct as is

   *b.* to eat, the farmer

   *c.* too eat, the farmer

   *d.* to eat. The farmer

7. Cowards are people who, when threatened, think with <u>their legs!</u>   **(10-d, 194)**

   *a.* Correct as is

   *b.* they're legs!

   *c.* there legs!

   *d.* they're legs.

8. In a battle, the octopus usually wins <u>due to its being well armed.</u>   **(35-c, 104)**

   *a.* Correct as is

   *b.* due to it's being well armed

   *c.* because it's well armed

   *d.* because its well armed

## PRACTICE SESSION 12—Capitalization

Which word in each set of parentheses is correct? (Review #206–219.)

1. He said brightly, "(a, A) house mouse can run up to four miles an hour." **(209-a)**

2. Ellen spilled Russian (dressing, Dressing) on her French fiancé. **(210-a.1)**

3. He said that (the, The) average bathtub holds 25 gallons of water. **(209-d)**

4. As they were traveling (south, South) on Route 1, she mentioned that travel broadens the mind and flattens the wallet! **(211-c)**

5. "An optimist," Jack said thoughtfully, "(is, Is) someone who takes a frying pan on a fishing trip." **(209-b)**

6. Because she is an astronomer, she named her ship (*white star*, *White Star*). **(210-b)**

7. A (junior, Junior) posted this ad: WANTED—TYPEWRITER TABLE FOR STUDENT WITH FOLDING LEGS. **(213-c)**

8. Fred Allen once defined a celebrity as "(a, A) person who works hard all his life to become well known, then wears dark glasses to avoid being recognized." **(209-c)**

9. Sign on a Merrydale (high school, High School) bulletin board: "Free every Monday through Friday—knowledge. Bring your own containers." **(213-a)**

10. In our town, the population of (protestants, Protestants), (catholics, Catholics), and (jews, Jews) is about equal. **(214-a)**

11. The cat joined the Red (cross, Cross) because it wanted to be a first-aid kit! **(212-a)**

12. On her (social studies, Social Studies) test, she wrote that all Spartan boys who could not walk were killed at birth. **(213-b)**

13. San Francisco is known for its sourdough bread, its cable cars, and its Golden Gate (bridge, Bridge). **(211-a)**

14. He's such a klutz mechanically that when he writes on his IBM (computer, Computer), he uses chalk! **(212-c)**

## PRACTICE SESSION 13—Mixed Bag

In each sentence find the error; understand it; correct it.

1. The last word in planes isnt the Concorde; it's jump!   **(226-a, 35-c)**

2. Sign in clothing store: 50% OFF! THESE TROUSERS LOOKS BETTER ON YOUR LEGS THAN ON OUR HANDS!   **(23-k, 47-b)**

3. If you want to kill time, why not try working it to death.   **(10-b)**

4. A lie traveling around the world while the truth is still putting on her boots!   **(12-b)**

5. I asked she and Eric what word can be pronounced quicker by adding a syllable to it. (Answer: quick.)   **(34-d.2)**

6. My brother he said that if you have a second to spare, he'll teach you all he knows!   **(37-b)**

7. One of Prince Charles' ancestors was George Washington another was Count Dracula.   **(222-a)**

8. Did you know that in Africa peanuts are called "goobers?"   **(225-g)**

9. According to one comedian, by the time a fellow has learned to read girls like a book, his liberry card has expired!   **(238)**

10. When a teacher in Merrydale high school asked what Caesar said when Brutus stabbed him, Timmy replied, "Ouch!"   **(213-a)**

11. One reason a buck won't do as much for people as it use to is that people won't do as much for a buck as they use to.   **(200)**

12. Who's never hungry at thanksgiving dinner? The turkey—it's stuffed!   **(210-d)**

13. That there fellow is called Tonsillitis because he's a pain in the neck!   **(196)**

14. "I am some smarter than my sister," she said, "especially in grammar."   **(189)**

15. "The writen word is more powerful than the sword," Pat said sharply.   **(237)**

16. Them excuses fooled no one but the person who made them.   **(37-d)**

17. Better days are coming—their called Saturday and Sunday!   **(194)**

## PRACTICE SESSION 14—Confused Words

Which word in parentheses is correct?

1. For fixing things around the house, nothing beats an owner (who's, whose) handy with a checkbook! **(204)**

2. Silly Suzy divided the pizza (among, between) the three hungry boys: half to Tom, half to Joe, and half to Bill. **(92)**

3. If you think you're a wit, (you're, your) half right! **(205)**

4. A farmer (passed, past) a small sports car and asked the driver: "Picked it before it was ripe, did you?" **(176)**

5. To a lazy friend, serve loaf cake for (desert, dessert)! **(121)**

6. We are not sure (weather, whether) splitting the atom was a wise crack! **(202)**

7. In 1789 George Washington, (famous, notorious) as our first President, had to borrow money to get to his inauguration. **(172)**

8. Read (farther, further) into the book and you will learn that, in ancient Sparta, overeating was punished by banishment. **(135)**

9. Yesterday my cat ate cheese and waited for the mouse with bated (breath, breathe). **(108)**

10. Television news doesn't make you (tearful, tearfull) if you don't turn it on! **(139)**

11. The one place where the U.S. flag flies (continually, continuously) without ever being raised or lowered is the moon. **(118)**

12. (Irregardless, Regardless) of what you say about crows, one thing is certain—they never complain without "caws"! **(153)**

13. The trouble with marriage is not the institution—it's the (personal, personnel)! **(178)**

14. A (real, really) good title for a book would be *The World of Sports* by Jim Nasium! **(184)**

15. When Jackie Gleason (saw, seen) Elvis Presley perform, he announced: "I tell you flatly—he won't last." **(186)**

16. The Washington Monument, a (historic, historical) structure, sinks six inches every year. **(148)**

*Laugh Your Way Through Grammar*

## PRACTICE SESSION 15—Agreement of Pronouns and Their Antecedents

Which pronoun in parentheses is correct? Why? (Review #36.)

1. Her family was unanimous in (its, their) definition of perpetual motion: the family living upstairs!   **(36-e)**

2. The only bright spot in some men's lives is on the seat of (his, their) pants!   **(36-a)**

3. Every teacher eventually realizes that (he or she has, they have) to take a roomful of live wires and make sure they're grounded!   **(36-d)**

4. No one has ever been bored by someone's paying (him or her, them) a compliment!   **(36-c)**

5. Neither of the boys wishes (his, their) doctor a prosperous New Year!   **(36-b)**

6. Melissa and Mamie rose before daylight to do (her, their) homework so that if they didn't know an answer, it would soon dawn on (her, them)!   **(36-f)**

7. Any parent will admit that what (he or she needs, they need) most is an automatic childwasher.   **(36-c, d)**

8. Everyone thinks that (he or she, they) had a wonderful vacation if (he or she, they) zipped through ten countries and $10,000 in two weeks! **(36-c)**

Sometimes the antecedent of a pronoun is not clear. How would you revise each of the following sentences to eliminate the ambiguity?   (See **#36-h**)

9. As soon as the surgeons left the operating rooms, the aides cleaned them.

10. When Jay and Greg were chatting, he learned that Beau Brummell, Abraham Lincoln, and Theodore Roosevelt were all great snorers!

11. The passengers in the two cars were taken to the hospital. They had collided on the Northway just north of Albany.

12. We unpacked the books from the cartons and then threw them out.

13. The detective trailed the suspect for hours before he hid in an old trash barrel.

## PRACTICE SESSION 16—Mixed Bag

Each sentence below contains an underlined expression. Below each sentence are four possible answers. Which one is correct?

1. Some people are like <u>french bread—little</u> dough but much crust.  **(210-a, 227-f)**
   - *a.* Correct as is
   - *b.* french bread, little
   - *c.* French bread—little
   - *d.* French bread. Little

2. The fruitcake was divided between <u>he and his sister:</u> he got the dough and she got the dates!  **(34-c, 223-b)**
   - *a.* Correct as is
   - *b.* him and his sister:
   - *c.* he and his sister,
   - *d.* him and his sister,

3. "I'd like four <u>loafs of rye,"</u> said the reformed alcoholic.  **(23-f, 225-g)**
   - *a.* Correct as is
   - *b.* loafs of rye",
   - *c.* loaves of rye",
   - *d.* loaves of rye,"

4. "A lame duck," said the history <u>teacher, "Is</u> a politician whose goose has been cooked."  **(209-b, 225-a)**
   - *a.* Correct as is
   - *b.* teacher, "is
   - *c.* teacher; "Is
   - *d.* teacher; is

5. Most of the world's great leaders have been fluent <u>speakers however</u> Aristotle stuttered.  **(74, 222-b)**
   - *a.* Correct as is
   - *b.* speakers, however,
   - *c.* speakers; however,
   - *d.* speakers; However,

6. "I'm going <u>nowhere!"</u> he said bleakly.  **(63-a, 229-b)**
   - *a.* Correct as is
   - *b.* nowhere"!
   - *c.* nowheres!"
   - *d.* nowheres"!

7. Shep Fields said a hick town is a place where "just three things happen—morning, noon, and <u>night"—which</u> amused me very much.  **(30-f, 227-f)**
   - *a.* Correct as is
   - *b.* night"—a description which
   - *c.* night." Which
   - *d.* night." A description which

8. A doctor is an angel when you're ill and a devil when <u>you're healthful</u> and her bill arrives.  **(147, 205)**
   - *a.* Correct as is
   - *b.* you're healthy
   - *c.* your healthful
   - *d.* your healthy

## PRACTICE SESSION 17—Verbs

Complete the following verse by providing the past tense form of each verb in parentheses. **(41-b)**

1. *(hang)*    A picture on the wall he __?__,
2. *(spring)*   From limb to limb she blithely __?__.
3. *(sting)*    The most amiable bee a baby __?__,
4. *(ring)*     And the bell in the steeple softly __?__.
5. *(swing)*    The chandelier from the ceiling __?__
6. *(sing)*     And the boys in the choir sweetly __?__.

Complete the following verse by providing the past tense form of each verb in parentheses in the first blank and the past participial form in the second. **(41-b)**

7. *(blow)*    She __?__ the glass, the glass was __?__,
8. *(throw)*   He __?__ the ball, the ball was __?__.

9. *(grow)*    She __?__ a foot, a foot she'd __?__,
10. *(know)*   The facts he __?__, the facts were __?__.

11. *(show)*   They __?__ the film, the film's been __?__,
12. *(fly)*    The birds __?__ south, the birds have __?__.

Which word or phrase in parentheses is correct? Why?

13. If you want to know the meaning of "difficult," (try and, try to) get a plumber on a weekend!   **(193)**

14. This sign (aggravated, irritated) me: NO—dogs/eating/bicycles.   **(82)**

15. In the past, confession (may have, may of) been good for the soul, but now it can be turned into a bestseller.   **(119)**

16. He (laid, lay) on the cot, as nervous as a clam at low tide.   **(159)**

17. "I (did, done) my homework, and I now know the principal parts of the verb 'do'."   **(126)**

18. Last year I (graduated, graduated from) college, but I'm still not very clever.   **(144)**

19. Old bankers never die: they just (loose, lose) interest!   **(166)**

## PRACTICE SESSION 18—Mixed Bag

Each sentence below contains an error. Find it; understand it; correct it.

1. Some ants lay around so much that the other ants kick them out of the colony.   **(159)**

2. If my son said what he thought he'd be speechless!   **(224-g, s)**

3. Always try and drive so that your license will expire before you do! **(193)**

4. Measles make me itch!   **(23-j)**

5. We all enjoyed Jerry reporting that germs are often caught on the fly!   **(50-c)**

6. She use to go to football games because she liked to see the fellows making passes.   **(200)**

7. Maureen, the more intelligent of the three girls, defined "cold cash" as money kept in an air-conditioned bank.   **(55-c)**

8. Our teacher wanted Bob and I to know that Helena, the capital of Montana, was once named "Last Chance Gulch."   **(48-f)**

9. Indigestion is the remorse of a guilty stomach, which a doctor told me.   **(30-f)**

10. (headline) TWO TEENAGE GIRLS ASSIGNED TO 100 HOURS OF COMMUNITY SERVICE ON TUESDAY NIGHT.   **(15-a.1)**

11. They're building faster planes and faster cars but they haven't yet come up with anything that goes faster than a buck!   **(224-f)**

12. This is a dogwood tree; you can tell by it's bark.   **(35-c)**

13. A hobo is like a balloon: neither has no visible means of support. **(63-c)**

14. Everyone trims off a branch occasionally when talking about their family tree!   **(36-c)**

15. An adult is someone who has ceased to grow vertically. But not horizontally!   **(12-d)**

16. A ship offen shows affection—it hugs the shore.   **(237)**

17. Among deers, the female is the boss . . . always.   **(23-i)**

## PRACTICE SESSION 19—Numbers

Each sentence below contains an error. Find it; understand it; correct it. (Review #239.)

1. On June 6 1987 Silly Suzy announced that the easiest way to make an egg roll is to push it.   **(239-g)**

2. Sign in pop rock music store on Forty-Third Street: TEENAGE SPOKEN HERE.   **(239-i)**

3. 20,000 men worked every day for twenty-two years to build the Taj Mahal in India.   **(239-e)**

4. The United States purchased Alaska for 2c an acre.   **(239-a)**

5. For the boys, sixty minutes are long enough to dress for a prom; for the girls, an hour is necessary.   **(239-k)**

6. To the weather forecaster, two plus two are four—probably.   **(239-l)**

7. One-half of the lies people tell isn't true!   **(239-j.4)**

8. She is 39; she has been for 8 years!   **(239-a)**

9. The weight of the Statue of Liberty is equal to that of 32 elephants, or six sperm whales, or 475 horses.   **(239-f)**

10. We purchased the Virgin Islands for two hundred and ninety-five dollars an acre.   **(239-b)**

11. "Just call me Bill," said one young fellow. "I was born on the 1st of the month."   **(239-d)**

12. Vanderbilt owes me one thousand two hundred and forty-six dollars and twenty-three cents.   **(239-b)**

13. Your chance of being injured in an aerobics class is one in two; of being hit by lightning, one in 600,000.   **(239-f)**

14. We found four 3s in the first problem.   **(239-h)**

15. On August twenty-second, nineteen hundred and two, Teddy Roosevelt was the first President to ride in an automobile.   **(239-g)**

16. Three dogs plus two cats are chaos!   **(239-l)**

17. I'm going to buy a farm two miles long and one half inch wide ... to raise spaghetti!   **(239-j.1)**

## PRACTICE SESSION 20—Mixed Bag

Each sentence below contains an underlined expression. Below each sentence are four possible answers. Which one is correct?

1. When Gullible Gus contradicts himself he's usually right. **(27, 224-g)**
   - *a.* Correct as is
   - *b.* hisself he's
   - *c.* himself, he's
   - *d.* hisself, he's

2. When Charles Dickens' novel, *Great Expectations*, was made into a movie, the Chinese version was called Bleeding tears of lonely star. **(216-b, 231-a)**
   - *a.* Correct as is
   - *b.* "Bleeding Tears of Lonely Star"
   - *c.* *Bleeding tears of lonely star*
   - *d.* *Bleeding Tears of Lonely Star*

3. A kindergarten teacher is someone who had ought to know how to make little things count! **(145, 30-d)**
   - *a.* Correct as is
   - *b.* whom had ought
   - *c.* who ought
   - *d.* whom ought

4. Grandpa Belden, setting in his rocker, muttered that the rising generation is a falling one. **(187, 224-j)**
   - *a.* Correct as is
   - *b.* Belden, sitting in his rocker,
   - *c.* Belden setting in his rocker
   - *d.* Belden, sitting in his rocker

5. My mother said I could become a lion tamer. **(37-b, 215-a)**
   - *a.* Correct as is
   - *b.* My Mother said
   - *c.* My Mother she said
   - *d.* My mother she said

6. A sentence 823 words long appears in Victor Hugo's novel *Les Miserables*. **(231-a)**
   - *a.* Correct as is
   - *b.* "Les Miserables".
   - *c.* "Les Miserables."
   - *d.* "Les Miserables".

7. The world seems to be made up of two kind of people: heroes and zeros. **(157, 23-e, 223-b)**
   - *a.* Correct as is
   - *b.* kinds of people: heroes
   - *c.* kinds of people; heroes
   - *d.* kind of people: heros

8. The barometer's falling; may be it wasn't nailed up right. **(169, 222-a)**
   - *a.* Correct as is
   - *b.* falling; maybe
   - *c.* falling, maybe
   - *d.* falling—may be

## PRACTICE SESSION 21—Parallel Structure

Which expression, *a* or *b*, is correct? (Review #20.)

1. He likes to ski, to hang-glide, and __?__.  **(20-g)**

   *(a)* having pretty girls sign his casts   *(b)* to have pretty girls sign his casts

2. It's a crime to catch a fish in some lakes and __?__ in others!  **(20-c)**

   *(a)* miraculous   *(b)* a miracle

3. Jack Kennedy liked coleslaw, Lyndon Johnson adored chili, and __?__.  **(20-a, f)**

   *(a)* Richard Nixon favored cottage cheese with catsup   *(b)* cottage cheese with catsup was a favorite of Richard Nixon

4. Parents are people who either are walking to reduce or __?__ to walking.  **(20-k)**

   *(a)* reduced   *(b)* are reduced

5. April is the month when the green returns both to the lawn and __?__!  **(20-j)**

   *(a)* the IRS   *(b)* to the IRS

6. Telling your troubles is __?__ your troubles.  **(20-h)**

   *(a)* swelling   *(b)* to swell

7. If one can water a horse, how come __?__ can't milk a cat?  **(20-d)**

   *(a)* one   *(b)* you

Be able to correct faulty parallel structure in the following sentences. Parallel items are italicized.

8. I lent money both *to a friend* and *an enemy*. (Result: two enemies and no friends!)  **(20-j)**

9. *To find* a place where the fish bite is easier than *finding* a place where the mosquitoes don't!  **(20-g)**

10. *Raining* cats and dogs isn't as bad as *to hail* buses and taxis.  **(20-h)**

11. Dogs can be *lonely*, *bored*, and sometimes *they become hysterically timid*.  **(20-i)**

## PRACTICE SESSION 22—Spelling and Confused Words

Test your spelling skill by completing each incomplete word in the sentences below. The three dots ( . . . ) may represent no letter, one letter, or two or three letters.

1. The princip. . . that honesty is the best policy will handicap you—especially in golf!  **(180, 238)**

2. The obstetrician rec. . .ved a license plate bearing the letters S T O R K.  **(234-c)**

3. He dis. . .pointed his mother when he gave up weight lifting for shoplifting.  **(232-a)**

4. The phrase, "robbing Peter to pay Paul," came into exist. . .ce in 1712 when English clergymen took the bells from the Church of St. Peter and hung them in the new St. Paul's Cathedral.  **(237)**

5. A college may be defined as a station. . .ry building with thousands of moving parts!  **(190)**

6. Silly Suzy said that the capit. . .l of Kentucky is "Hot Dog."  **(113)**

7. The greatest unemployment al. . .ready exists in the area north of the ears!  **(90)**

8. What books are most . . .ffected by hard times? Pocketbooks!  **(81)**

9. You need a large purse to compl. . .ment that new suit—and to pay for it!  **(116)**

10. There's a new diet that will final. . .y help millions of Americans to lose weight: the high price of food!  **(233-a)**

11. Temper is a funny thing; you can't get rid of it by lo. . .sing it.  **(166, 233-b)**

12. In the woods we picnic. . .ed, ending with watermelon: a fruit you can eat, drink, and wash your face in.  **(236)**

13. After stud. . .ing the matter, she announced that an egotist is someone who is always me-deep in conversation!  **(235-a)**

14. If exerci. . .e is so good for us, why do so many ath. . .letes retire at thirty-five?  **(237)**

15. According to Simple Simon, the largest veg. . .table is a police officer's "beet."  **(237)**

*Laugh Your Way Through Grammar*

# PRACTICE SESSION 23—Mixed Bag

In each sentence there are three underlined words or phrases. Which *one* of the three contains an error in grammar, spelling, usage, or punctuation?

1. Why <u>don't</u> you close that mouth of <u>your's</u>? I feel a <u>draft</u>!  **(35-b)**

2. <u>Every one</u> uses sign <u>language</u> these <u>days:</u> we sign for everything we buy.  **(134)**

3. The Lose-It-Now Club <u>were</u> eager to <u>accept</u> as a <u>motto—"The best way to reduce is to keep your mouth shut!"</u>  **(47-q)**

4. <u>Us</u> tourists discovered that <u>Amsterdam</u> has 636 bridges, more <u>than any other city</u> in the world.  **(37-c)**

5. Math teacher: "If I slide down this hill four feet a <u>second, what will</u> be my condition at the end of <u>twenty five</u> seconds?"
   Student: "<u>You'll</u> be a centipede."  **(239-a)**

6. After he won a million <u>dollars,</u> he was stunned at the <u>amount</u> of friends he had suddenly <u>acquired</u>!  **(93)**

7. I <u>can not</u> deny that I was shocked when I read this <u>headline: SHOOT</u> KIDS TO STOP <u>MEASLES</u>.  **(111)**

8. <u>There</u> would be <u>less</u> pedestrian <u>patients</u> if there were more patient pedestrians!  **(136)**

9. Abigail <u>Adams, wife</u> of <u>President</u> John Adams, <u>hanged</u> the family washing in the East Room of the White House.  **(146)**

10. If he had asked, I <u>would of</u> reminded him that if you <u>lie</u> down with <u>dogs, you'll</u> get up with fleas.  **(119)**

11. When the customer complained that he hadn't found any ham in his <u>sandwich, the</u> waiter said <u>consolingly, "You</u> must have gone right <u>passed it!"</u>  **(176.1)**

12. Be <u>sure and</u> write about the largest popsicle ever <u>made; it</u> weighed <u>5,750</u> pounds.  **(193)**

13. Some of <u>these here</u> turkey gobblers would strut <u>less</u> if they could look <u>into</u> the future.  **(196)**

14. I saw in a book <u>where</u> a <u>snail's</u> pace is about <u>two inches</u> a minute.  **(75-f)**

## PRACTICE SESSION 24—Agreement of Subject and Verb

From the words in parentheses, select the correct verb form. (Review #47.)

1. One thing that you can always count on (are, is)—your fingers! **(47-b)**

2. In school neither Abraham Lincoln nor Henry Ford (was, were) especially promising.   **(47-f )**

3. The dumbwaiter, as well as waffles, (was, were) introduced by Thomas Jefferson.   **(47-k)**

4. According to those who should know, there (are, is)—in the Eiffel Tower—2,500,000 rivets.   **(47-s)**

5. Grandpa claims that everyone who sings rock (are, is) long on hair and short on talent.   **(47-l)**

6. One of the amazing things (are, is) that plastic wrap clings to the roll but not to the bowl!   **(47-h)**

7. Plenty of sour pickles (are, is) in the picnic basket.   **(47-i)**

8. She is the one of the girls in her group who (find, finds) ice-skating a sedentary sport!   **(47-j)**

9. Of course carrots and cabbage (are, is) good for the eyes! Have you ever seen a rabbit with glasses?   **(47-d)**

10. Bad news (fly, flies) faster than sound!   **(47-c)**

11. Whenever Gullible Gus (want, wants) to have a big time in the city, he wears a large watch!   **(47-a)**

12. The number of cars with clever license plates (are, is) increasing. My favorite is the army jeep with the number HUP 234!   **(47-p)**

13. According to my uncle, one of the world's best after-dinner speeches (are, is)—"I'll take both checks, waiter."   **(47-h)**

14. Neither her sisters nor Julie (repeat, repeats) rumors—all three create them!   **(47-g)**

15. Few of the people I know (want, wants) to admit that the easiest thing to run into is debt.   **(29-b, 47-h, l)**

## PRACTICE SESSION 25—Mixed Bag

In each pair of sentences below, one is correct and one is incorrect. Which is which? Why?

1. (a) Eating only one peanut takes more courage than to face a pride of lions!

   (b) Eating only one peanut takes more courage than facing a pride of lions! **(20-h)**

2. (a) At that delicatessen, you will find many fine foods served by experienced waitresses in appetizing forms.

   (b) At that delicatessen, you will find many fine foods in appetizing forms served by experienced waitresses. **(15-a)**

3. (a) "All the tea in China" is about 370,000 tons a year, a fact which amazes me.

   (b) "All the tea in China" is about 370,000 tons a year, which amazes me. **(30-f)**

4. (a) When Luis was four, his father played for the New York Yankees.

   (b) His father, when he was four, played for the New York Yankees. **(36-h.1)**

5. (a) Parents of a teenage boy always know their son is in the car, but they usually don't know where the car is!

   (b) Parents of a teenage boy always know their son is in the car, but the whereabouts of the car is usually unknown! **(45-c)**

6. (a) Submit a travel voucher with the receipts attached to your school principal.

   (b) Submit to your school principal a travel voucher with the receipts attached. **(15-a)**

7. (a) When you make a pun, it earns you groans from your listeners!

   (b) Making a pun earns you groans from your listeners! **(155)**

8. (a) While he was with Commodore Perry in Japan in 1854, Jonathan Goble, a U.S. Marine, invented the rickshaw.

   (b) While he was with Commodore Perry in Japan in 1854, the rickshaw was invented by Jonathan Goble, a U.S. Marine. **(45-c)**

## PRACTICE SESSION 26—Mixed Bag

Each sentence below contains an error. Find it; understand it; correct it.

1. If mistakes learn you to think, you're getting a fantastic education! **(161)**

2. An elephant don't eat peanuts in the jungle; it has to be taught to like them. **(127)**

3. Either "Adam and Eve on a raft" (poached eggs on toast) or "Wreck 'em" (scrambled eggs) are my favorite example of waiters' slang. **(47-f)**

4. When you get your hospital bill, you understood why surgeons wear masks in the operating room! **(20-e)**

5. She cooked herself an omelet, then read the newspaper while eating it. **(36-h.2)**

6. If I would have gone to the hospital, both my checkbook and I would be on the critical list! **(46-c.2)**

7. Silly Suzy said solemnly that floods from the Mississippi river can be prevented by putting big "dames" in the river. **(211-a)**

8. Mark Twain's Life on the Mississippi was the first typewritten book manuscript sent to a publisher. **(231-a)**

9. Lyndon Johnson said there are two kinds of speeches: the first, the Mother Hubbard speech, covers everything but touches nothing, the second, the Bikini speech, covers only the essential points. **(222-a, c)**

10. Disgruntled, he described the English Department in his high school as a "Chamber of Commas". **(225-g.1)**

11. Morty definitely benefitted from a knowledge of the old proverb: "Many a man's tongue has broken his nose." **(233-d)**

12. A apple a day may keep the doctor away, but a onion a day will keep everybody away! **(56-g)**

13. I don't see no reason for the rule against double negatives. **(63-c)**

14. Love is one game you can't call due to darkness. **(104)**

15. Two cupsful of honey cannot sweeten a friend's angry words. **(23-m)**

## PRACTICE SESSION 27—Use of Commas

The following sentences need commas. (The number needed is indicated in brackets.) Where should the commas be inserted? Why? (Review #224.)

1. Jim if Adam returned to earth the only thing he'd recognize would be your jokes! [2]   **(224-g, n)**

2. In ancient Rome it was a common practice to dye a mustache blue green or orange. [2]   **(224-c)**

3. The night falls but never breaks and the day breaks but never falls. [1] **(224-f)**

4. Well you might say a sentence is something that ends with a period or a parole! [1]   **(224-o)**

5. Vatican City Monaco and the eight-square-mile Pacific island of Nauru are the three smallest countries in the world. [2]   **(224-a)**

6. "I run things at my house" he said as he switched on the washer the vacuum cleaner and the microwave. [3]   **(224-a, r)**

7. What she most enjoys she complains is always illegal immoral or fattening. [4]   **(224-c, p)**

8. After lasting 150 days the most determined eyelash dies. [1]   **(224-h)**

9. Both John Adams and Thomas Jefferson died on July 4 1826. [1] **(224-q)**

10. He practiced telling jokes on his friends on his teachers and even on his own reflection in the mirror! [2]   **(224-e)**

11. A lover tells lies a seer tells fortunes and a child tells everything! [2] **(224-d)**

12. He went to the races made a mental bet and lost his mind! [2] **(224-b)**

13. What happens Ellen when the smog lifts over Los Angeles? (Answer: U C L A—you see L.A.) [2]   **(224-n)**

14. Using round rocks for balls and pointed stones for pins Egyptian children "bowled" 7,000 years ago! [1]   **(224-i.2)**

15. It is dangerous to go into the woods in the spring because the grass has blades the flowers have pistils and the leaves shoot! [2]   **(224-d)**

## PRACTICE SESSION 28—Punctuation

What punctuation marks are needed in the following sentences? (The number required is in brackets.)

1. Horse sense of course dwells in a stable mind. [2]　**(224-p)**

2. Whenever you can hang around lucky people. [1]　**(224-s)**

3. Ambrose Bierce humorist and cynic called the Presidency a "greased pig in the field of American politics." [2]　**(224-m)**

4. James Garfield who was our twentieth President could write Latin with one hand and Greek with the other simultaneously! [3]　**(224-l, 227-d)**

5. To eat is human to digest divine. [2]　**(222-a, 224-t)**

6. A half-minute—that's a thirty second slot for a TV commercial may sell for as high as $400,000! [2]　**(227-b, 230-a)**

7. The odds against a diet's succeeding are three to one knife fork and spoon. [3]　**(223-a, 224-a)**

8. To Carol Crosby was the greatest singer of all time. [1]　**(224-s)**

9. If you wish to wear your new dress. [1]　**(224-s)**

10. The phrase "down in the dumps" may have originated with Dumpos a King of Egypt who built a pyramid but died of melancholy. [1] **(224-m)**

11. Sammy Davis Jr. once said "Fame creates its own standards. A guy who twitches his lips is just another guy with a lip twitch unless he's Humphrey Bogart." [3]　**(223-c, 224-w)**

12. Fleas are arithmetic bugs they add to your misery subtract from your pleasure divide your attention and multiply like the dickens. [4] **(223-b, 224-b)**

13. Yes our national flower should be the concrete cloverleaf! [1] **(224-o)**

14. Kurt Vonnegut the American novelist once called New York "Skyscraper National Park." [2]　**(224-m)**

15. If fortune hands you a lemon squeeze it sweeten it and enjoy it as lemonade. [3]　**(224-d, g)**

## PRACTICE SESSION 29—Mixed Bag

In each sentence there are three underlined words or phrases. Which *one* of the three contains an error in grammar, spelling, usage, or punctuation? Why?

1. The <u>library</u> is the tallest building in <u>town:</u> it has <u>alot</u> of stories!   **(89)**

2. When she tripped over her own <u>foot,</u> she was so <u>mad</u> she tried to sue <u>herself!</u>   **(95)**

3. Both Clarissa and <u>myself</u> know that "as quick as a <u>wink</u>" is <u>three-tenths</u> of a second.   **(27-c)**

4. The <u>president</u> of the firm told <u>she</u> and her sister that the average pencil can draw a line <u>thirty-five</u> miles long!   **(34-b)**

5. A disc jockey moves <u>more fast</u> than most people because <u>he's</u> living on "spins" and <u>needles.</u>   **(62-b)**

6. <u>Him</u> suggesting they have a battle of wits caused her to <u>murmur:</u> "How brave of you to fight <u>unarmed!</u>"   **(50-c)**

7. Twenty <u>dollars worth</u> of groceries once filled the car <u>trunk;</u> now it fills the glove <u>compartment!</u>   **(226-d)**

8. She's a <u>women</u> who suffers for her <u>beliefs:</u> she believes she can wear a size <u>five shoe</u> on a size nine foot!   **(23-h)**

9. I agree with <u>whomever</u> said that a <u>college</u> education is the one thing some people are willing to pay <u>for—and</u> not get.   **(69-c)**

10. A <u>bachelor's</u> apartment is one <u>in which</u> the only thing <u>hanged</u> up neatly is the telephone!   **(146)**

11. <u>Gossip,</u> like <u>grapefruit,</u> has <u>got</u> to be juicy to be good.   **(143)**

12. "This pair of scissors <u>need</u> sharpening," <u>my</u> mother said <u>dully.</u>   **(174)**

13. From his cooking, we <u>imply</u> that the <u>chef's</u> favorite <u>country</u> is—Greece!   **(150)**

14. The <u>Ex-President</u> said jokingly that when Alaska became the forty-ninth <u>state, Americans</u> got the biggest snow job in <u>history!</u>   **(210-a.4, 215-b)**

15. Pulling up a tree by its <u>roots, was</u> child's play for <u>Wonder Woman</u> when she was <u>three years old.</u>   **(224-x)**

## PRACTICE SESSION 30—Mixed Bag

Each sentence below contains an underlined expression. Below each sentence are four possible answers. Which one is correct?

1. When a customer asked if crabs were served, the waiter smiled. "We try and serve anyone, sir." **(98, 193)**

   *a.* Correct as is
   *b.* try and serve any one,
   *c.* try to serve any one,
   *d.* try to serve anyone,

2. A lot of indigestion is caused by people having to eat up their own words. **(194, 199)**

   *a.* Correct as is
   *b.* eat up they're
   *c.* eat there
   *d.* eat their

3. Doctor, do you think cranberries are healthy? Well, I've never heard one complain. **(147, 207, 224-o)**.

   *a.* Correct as is
   *b.* healthful, well,
   *c.* healthful? Well,
   *d.* healthy—well,

4. If you hear an owl hoot "To whom" instead of "To who," you can be sure you are in Boston, the capitol of Massachusetts. **(113, 224-m)**

   *a.* Correct as is
   *b.* Boston, the capital
   *c.* Boston; the capital
   *d.* Boston—the capitol

5. It's alright to drink like a fish if you drink what a fish does! **(35-c, 91)**

   *a.* Correct as is
   *b.* Its alright
   *c.* It's all right
   *d.* Its all right

6. "Knuckle" used to mean "knee joint, and falling to one's knees to avoid punishment resulted in the phrase, "to knuckle under." **(224-f; 225-b)**

   *a.* Correct as is
   *b.* joint," and
   *c.* joint" and
   *d.* joint": and

7. Vic is lazier than me—he aims at nothing and hits it. **(37-a, 195)**

   *a.* Correct as is
   *b.* then me;
   *c.* then I;
   *d.* than I—

8. When Andrew Jackson left the White House, he had only $90 in cash. **(63-g, 224-g)**

   *a.* Correct as is
   *b.* House, he only had
   *c.* house; he only had
   *d.* House—he had only

## PRACTICE SESSION 31—Mixed Bag

In each sentence find the error; understand it; correct it.

1. "Guess I'll hit the hay," said the farmer as he slid off of the barn. **(69-a)**

2. You could of kept the milk from turning sour if you had kept it in the cow. **(119)**

3. The jury gave the judge their verdict: "We don't want to get involved." **(36-e)**

4. When the King of England came up to the White House for dinner, Eleanor Roosevelt cheerfully served hot dogs. **(199)**

5. The White House was compared with a jail by George Washington, Warren Harding, and Harry Truman. **(115)**

6. In Texas, a pig named Ralph not only dives and swims but also it does tricks underwater. **(171)**

7. A hospital is where people who are run down wind up. **(154)**

8. Some of the wealthy are like bagels, nothing surrounded by dough! **(227-d)**

9. Don't blame it on me that the children are running everything around the house except errands! **(69-a, 155)**

10. I told her the two most beautiful words in the English language are "Check enclosed." Hopefully she'll now return my $10! **(149)**

11. When the warden asked the prisoners what kind of a party they'd like, they suggested an Open House. **(156)**

12. Neither his sister nor Jack misbehave on the farm; they know the potatoes have eyes and the corn has ears! **(47-f)**

13. When she went on a diet, she must of realized that the hardest meal to skip is—the next one! **(119)**

14. There's a man outside with a wooden leg named Smith. **(15-c)**

15. The best place to quickly find a helping hand is at the end of your arm. **(48-a)**

16. A book in the hand is worth two in the liberry. **(237, 238)**

Each sentence below contains an error. Find it; understand it; correct it.

1. Of all dogs, a bloodhound is the more intelligent because it earns its own living by picking up a few ''scents'' a day!  **(55-c)**

2. Father disapproved of me sleeping behind the wheel.  **(50-c)**

3. They sure get along like brothers—Cain and Abel!  **(192)**

4. (alibi by a speeder) This highway is so dangerous I was hurrying to get off of it.  **(69-a)**

5. He boasted that he has an open mind, but it was merely vacant!  **(40-a)**

6. Leave a convict have enough rope and he'll skip!  **(162)**

7. A pack of TV comics are like a pack of crackerjacks: some nuts and lots of corn!  **(47-q.1, 3)**

8. Louisa and me discovered that it is possible to skate on thin ice and end up in hot water!  **(33-b)**

9. You may sometimes use dashs to separate a parenthetical expression from the rest of the sentence.  **(23-a)**

10. You could put all the people in the world into a box one mile high, one mile wide, and one mile long; and then you could put that box inside of the Grand Canyon!  **(152)**

11. Baseball is one game that cannot be played good without an occasional sacrifice.  **(141)**

12. If anyone claims that raising a family is like playing golf, they mean they can do a better job next time.  **(36-b, c)**

13. Silly Suzy says this song is in the key of C because it has neither ''sharks'' or ''flaps.''  **(36-g)**

14. It was Henry Sigerist who placed a hospital somewheres between a ''penitentiary and a third-class hotel.''  **(63-a)**

15. Children are no different than other people—just shorter.  **(123)**

16. It's worth selling your last shirt to become a millionaire, which is an interesting thought!  **(30-f)**

## PRACTICE SESSION 33—Redundancies

A redundant word or expression exists in each of the following sentences. Identify each; be able to correct the sentence. (Review #240.)

1. Learning past history is easy; learning its lessons is almost impossible.

2. Among the new innovations introduced by Benjamin Franklin was toothpaste made from crushed charcoal mixed with honey.

3. In the early beginning, the winning baseball team was the one that first made twenty-one runs.

4. Silly Suzy wanted the biggest and largest jewel in the world, so she asked for a baseball diamond!

5. If you repeat the word "nerd" again, you will receive an "F" in English!

6. The cheapest and most economical way to have your family tree traced is to run for office!

7. The trouble is that the modern car of tomorrow is being driven on the highway of yesterday by the driver of today.

8. We have so many auto accidents in our town that our hospital refers back to its accident cases as its bumper crop.

9. Reincarnation: five p.m. in the afternoon when all the dead people come to life!

10. There's a new rice diet that is guaranteed to make you lose weight: you use only one single chopstick!

11. The spare tire around your waist may possibly be the most expensive one you can buy.

12. Christopher Morley christened his kittens as "Shall" and "Will" because so few people could tell them apart!

13. Visitor: "You're prettier in appearance than your mother." Little girl: "I should be. I'm a later model."

14. Cross a carrier pigeon and a woodpecker, and the end result is a bird that can not only carry messages but also knock on the door when it arrives.

## PRACTICE SESSION 34—Mixed Bag

Which word in each set of parentheses is correct?

1. If you insist on having a place in the sun, (you're, your) going to get some blisters! **(205)**

2. She bought plastic sheet music (so, so that) she could sing in the shower! **(75-g)**

3. A sign at a missile (sight, site) states boldly: "Out to launch!" **(114)**

4. She is (quiet, quite) sure the new play has a happy ending because, she says, everyone is glad it is over! **(182)**

5. A banker (lends, loans) you an umbrella when the sun is shining and wants it back the minute it begins to rain. **(163)**

6. If I (was, were) a mouse, I'd laugh at a cat only when I was near a hole. **(46-c)**

7. Our new baby (had ought, ought) to be called the Prince of "Wails." **(145)**

8. The early North American Indians made a mistake by not having an (emigration, immigration) bureau! **(130)**

9. Appearances can be deceptive: a dollar bill looks just (as, like) it did twenty years ago. **(165)**

10. One Hollywood star (who, whom) hasn't been spoiled is Mickey Mouse! **(30-d.1)**

11. Frequently when a hyena is attacked, it (lays, lies) down and plays dead. **(159)**

12. He is always (forgeting, forgetting) that while some fools make money, money also makes some fools! **(233-d)**

13. Either of the hotels (are, is) satisfactory for a change and a rest: the bellboys get the change and the hotel gets the rest! **(36-b, 47-h)**

14. From the cookbook, it was easy to (imply, infer) that a pickle is merely a cucumber made sour by a jarring experience! **(150)**

15. The (eminent, imminent) restaurant owner told us that, years ago, when a customer ordered corned beef hash, the waiter shouted to the chef, "Sweep up the kitchen!" **(131)**

## PRACTICE SESSION 35—Mixed Bag

In each sentence there are three underlined words or phrases. Which *one* of the three contains an error in grammar, spelling, usage, or punctuation?

1. The modern idea of roughing it is to have <u>only</u> three <u>radioes</u> in <u>one's</u> tent!   **(23-d)**

2. He <u>isnt</u> a player for the <u>Tigers;</u> <u>he's</u> still a Cub.   **(226-a)**

3. Of the two <u>women,</u> May is the <u>smartest</u> because she knows that it is not the <u>I.Q.</u> but the I WILL that is important.   **(55-b)**

4. Here is a toast you don't <u>never</u> make to a boat <u>crew</u>— <u>"Bottoms up!"</u>   **(63-c)**

5. As you walk <u>in</u> the future, <u>don't</u> be <u>tardy,</u> or it will be gone before you get there!   **(151)**

6. It was <u>him</u> who said that some people fashion <u>their</u> lives after French <u>bread—one</u> long loaf!   **(33-d)**

7. She <u>done</u> <u>weight</u> lifting with the wrong <u>equipment:</u> a knife and a fork.   **(126)**

8. Each of <u>almost</u> a million Americans <u>drink</u> <u>Coca-Cola</u> for breakfast.   **(47-h)**

9. Someone (<u>could it have been Sam Goldwyn</u>) once <u>said,</u> "Include <u>me out.</u>"   **(221-b)**

10. Since the game of Monopoly came into <u>existence in 1932</u> more than <u>2½ billion</u> little green <u>houses have been made.</u>   **(224-g)**

11. Detroit is working on <u>its</u> biggest <u>new</u> innovation in <u>years</u>—a windshield wiper that won't hold parking tickets!   **(240)**

12. Some <u>Americans</u> think it is <u>alright</u> to use <u>their</u> imagination when making out income tax returns.   **(91)**

13. A <u>neighboring</u> farmer ran a steamroller over his <u>field</u> because he wanted to raise <u>less</u> baked potatoes and more mashed potatoes!   **(136)**

14. "I shall be very glad to lend you my lawnmower," said Mark Twain, "but since I make it a rule never to <u>leave</u> it <u>leave</u> my lawn, you will be obliged to use it <u>there.</u>"   **(162)**

15. Rover is the sort <u>of a dog</u> that <u>drops out</u> of <u>obedience</u> school.   **(156)**

## PRACTICE SESSION 36—Confused Words

Which word in parentheses should fill the blank?

1. **(peace, piece)**  Russia says she wants __?__ in Asia and Africa, but doesn't say how big a __?__.  **(177)**

2. **(to, too, two)**  Vacation: It consists of __?__ weeks which are __?__ short, after which you are __?__ tired __?__ return __?__ work and __?__ broke not __?__.  **(198)**

3. **(their, there, they're)**  __?__ are some people who attend church only three times in __?__ lives: when __?__ hatched, when __?__ matched, and when __?__ dispatched.  **(194)**

4. **(your, you're)**  If __?__ going to complain about farmers, don't talk with __?__ mouth full.  **(205)**

5. **(council, counsel)**  The best __?__ is only as good as the use a __?__ makes of it.  **(120)**

6. **(disinterested, uninterested)**  A rabid baseball fan yearns for a(n) __?__ umpire and a(n) __?__ wife!  **(125)**

7. **(raise, rise)**  It is necessary to __?__ dough if you wish to have dough __?__.  **(183)**

8. **(borrow, lend, loan)**  Bank interest on a __?__ is so high that if you can afford to pay it, you don't need to __?__ money—you could __?__ them some!  **(163)**

9. **(advice, advise)**  I must __?__ you that giving good __?__ does not qualify as charity!  **(80)**

10. **(liable, likely)**  If you drive faster than the speed limit, you are __?__ to avoid being late but are __?__ to lose your license.  **(164)**

11. **(bring, take)**  I am going to __?__ my dog to obedience school so that I can __?__ home a dog with a "pet degree"!  **(109)**

12. **(angel, angle)**  The Broadway __?__ has an unusual __?__: to plant an ounce of seed money and harvest a ton of corn!  **(94)**

13. **(allusion, illusion)**  When she makes __?__s to her friendships with Princess Di, Michael Fox, and Stephen King, I know she's suffering from __?__s regarding her own importance!  **(87)**

# PRACTICE SESSION 37 — Sentence Combining

Be able to combine each cluster of sentences below into one good sentence. The reference numbers suggest possible methods.

1. Minister: "Do you say prayers before eating?"
   Small boy: "We don't have to. Mom's a good cook." **(21-i)**

2. In 1943 Thomas J. Watson was Chairman of the Board of International Business Machines. He once noted: "I think there is a world market for about five computers." **(21-a)**

3. A teenager had a spoiled little sister. He was asked if he played a musical instrument. "Only second fiddle at home," he replied. **(21-b and i)**

4. Blue eyes are most sensitive to pain. After blue, in descending order, are hazel, green, brown, and dark brown. **(21-h)**

5. A "glitch" was once an electronic or mechanical failure. Now it is used to name any error or minor mishap. **(21-a)**

6. There's one sure way to have a few minutes of solitude. Just start doing the dishes! **(21-c)**

7. Motorist: "My Jaguar hit a pig and turned turtle."
   Garage mechanic: "This is a garage, not a zoo!" **(21-i)**

8. Enrico Caruso was a great Italian tenor. He was discouraged by his first singing teacher. The teacher said that Caruso's voice was like "wind whistling through a window." **(21-a and i)**

9. Preservatives can be dangerous. Food coloring can be dangerous. Also dangerous are cholesterol and calories. Perhaps the only way to survive is to starve to death! **(21-e and h)**

10. Thomas Edison invented wax paper. He also invented the flashlight. The voting machine is another of his inventions. **(21-g)**

11. They say you should deal with a bank you can trust. Then you walk into a bank and find all the pens are chained to the counters! **(21-j)**

12. In 1969, in Vietnam, the U.S. Army drafted cats to guide soldiers on night missions. It didn't work. The cats guided the soldiers to mice and birds and ran away when it rained. **(21-j)**

## PRACTICE SESSION 38 — Mixed Bag

In each group of sentences below, the same idea is expressed in four different ways. For *each* group, select the way that is best.

1. (*a*) I don't like baking cookies as much as I like eating them.
   (*b*) I don't like to bake cookies as much as I like eating them.
   (*c*) I don't like baking cookies as much as I like to eat them.
   (*d*) I don't like to bake cookies as much as I like sitting down to eat them.

2. (*a*) I wouldn't of gone to the bakery if I hadn't "kneaded" the dough.
   (*b*) I wouldn't have gone to the bakery if I hadn't "kneaded" the dough.
   (*c*) I wouldn't have went to the bakery if I hadn't "kneaded" the dough.
   (*d*) I wouldn't of went to the bakery if I hadn't "kneaded" the dough.

3. (*a*) It is better to, I think, have character than to be one.
   (*b*) It is better to, I think, have character than being one.
   (*c*) Having character, I think, is better than to be one.
   (*d*) It is better, I think, to have character than to be one.

4. (*a*) TV replaced not only radio but also homework.
   (*b*) Not only did TV replace radio but homework also.
   (*c*) TV not only replaced radio but also homework.
   (*d*) TV not only replaced radio but homework also.

5. (*a*) In 1948 the comic strip *Bringing Up Father* used a secret code to alert investors to either buy or to sell certain stocks.
   (*b*) In 1948 the comic strip *Bringing Up Father* used a secret code to alert investors either to buy or sell certain stocks.
   (*c*) In 1948 the comic strip *Bringing Up Father* used a secret code either to alert investors to buy or to sell certain stocks.
   (*d*) In 1948 the comic strip *Bringing Up Father* used a secret code to alert investors either to buy or to sell certain stocks.

6. (*a*) Singing "Take Me Out to the Ballgame," the bus full of seniors left at 9 a.m. for Shea Stadium.
   (*b*) Singing "Take Me Out to the Ballgame," the senior bus left at 9 a.m. for Shea Stadium.
   (*c*) Singing "Take Me Out to the Ballgame," the seniors left in a bus at 9 a.m. for Shea Stadium.
   (*d*) Singing "Take Me Out to the Ballgame," Shea Stadium was the destination for the senior bus that left at 9 a.m.

## PRACTICE SESSION 39 — Mixed Bag

Each of the sentences below contains two (or possibly more) errors. Find them; identify them; correct them.

1. I never beleived I'd see the day when there'd be more blue jeans on Broadway then in Kansas!

2. Vivian read in the *Merrydale Daily* times where the glue on each postage stamp contains only one-tenth of a calorie.

3. I wish to say to whomever is interested that "A" is a letter thats always written in hAste!

4. The most noblest of all dogs is the hot dog, it feeds the hand that bites it!

5. According to Christopher Morley, their are three ingredients in the good life, learning, earning, and yearning.

6. A very perfect example of minority rule, is a baby in the house.

7. You spilling the salt may be bad luck, but if you spill the beans, it's downright dangerous!

8. Russian dressing is unknown in Russia, and practically unknown in England is the muffin called a English muffin.

9. Before I part with you, let me remind you that a tongue four inches long can kill a person six foot tall.

10. According to one boy scout I know, pound for pound the Shetland pony is stronger than any horse in the world.

11. I never file a tax return without I remember that the US was founded to AVOID taxation.

12. After saying "All that glitters is not gold," the sham bracelet was returned back to the jeweler's tray.

13. When Junior said he had failed his geography test because he couldn't remember where the Himalayas were, his father replied: "Next time remember where you put you're things!"

14. Heaped high with whipped cream and pink roses the bride nibbled on a peice of the wedding cake.

## PRACTICE SESSION 40 — Mixed Bag

Each of the first five sentences contains two (or possibly more) errors. Find them; identify them; correct them.

1. Three things smell badly: rotten eggs, spoiled fish, and visitors which stay too long.

2. If I was President of the U.S., I would ask people to drive careful: Uncle Sam needs every taxpayer he can get!

3. You won't get your toes stepped on at work without youre standing still or sitting down on the job.

4. Mom told my sister and I to always remember to staple shut the tops of potato chip bags.

5. It was Copernicus whom, according to historians, taught that the Earth revolved around the Sun.

In each pair of sentences below, one is correct and one is incorrect. Which is which? Why?

6. (a) As he entered the forest, he quickly spotted magnificently antlered elks and chipmunks.
   (b) As he entered the forest, he quickly spotted chipmunks and magnificently antlered elks.

7. (a) When crossing a desert, you should carry a watch because it has a spring in it!
   (b) When crossing a desert, a watch should be carried because it has a spring in it!

8. (a) When you find a pin, it's supposed to mean that you will have good luck.
   (b) Finding a pin is supposed to mean that you will have good luck.

9. (a) "Why don't you go forth and multiply?" Noah impatiently asked the two snakes. "We can't," they said. "We're adders."
   (b) "Why don't you go forth and multiply?" Noah impatiently asked the two snakes.
   "We can't," they said. "We're adders."

10. (a) A rabbit takes not only eighteen naps a day but also doesn't perspire.
    (b) A rabbit not only takes eighteen naps a day but also doesn't perspire.

# PRACTICE SESSION 41 — Mixed Bag

Each of the sentences below contains two (or possibly more) errors. Find them; identify them; correct them.

1. As most of our citizens knows, there would be less criminals if we could get more cops off television and onto the streets.

2. I had already took a taxi in Tokyo before I learned that that city has the worse traffic jams in the world.

3. A most unique word is "googol." The name of the figure "one" followed by 100 zeros.

4. When the teacher said he failed English, the little boy complained: "The teaching machine don't like me!"

5. Acting more friendlier than usual, Milly invited Vicki and I to meet a psychiatrist—that is, a mind-sweeper!

6. An extraordinary amount of potholes scar U.S. roads—almost fifty-six millions!

7. My uncle is richer than anyone: instead of wearing glasses, a prescription windshield was installed in his Cadillac!

8. Neither of my friends believe that the only way to be healthful is to cat what you don't likc!

9. Television is never liable to take the place of newspapers; you can't use TV to swat a fly, to train a dog, or for wrapping up garbage.

10. Johnny brung to the teacher this question: Which is more correct—six octopuses or six octopi? (Answer: either is correct.)

11. The five vowels—a, e, i, o, u—only appear in their proper order in two English words. AbstEmIOUs and fAcEtIOUs.

12. The child's toys, a doll, a whistling top, a robot, and a tea set, all laid broken on the floor of the nursery.

13. Babies pacifiers are really plugs: they kept screams in and thumbs out!

14. Neither the wife who drives from the back seat or the husband who cooks from the table know the secret of a happy marriage.

15. If you hope to adopt successfully to life in Sweden, be punctual both for business and social engagements.

## PRACTICE SESSION 42 — Pronoun Roundup

Which word in parentheses is correct? Why?

1. When the lawyer asked his secretary if the grand jury had returned an indictment, she asked: "(Who, Whom) did they borrow it from?"

2. (Whoever, Whomever) steals your watch should be known as "Procrastinator," the thief of time!

3. They offered to hire (whoever, whomever) had the longest fingernails!

4. Wife: If this ship sinks, (who, whom) would you save first—the children or me?
   Husband: Me.

5. I agree with (whoever, whomever) it was who said a book in the hand is worth two in the library!

6. (Who, Whom) did you say is more mixed up than a plate of spaghetti?

7. (Who, Whom) were you addressing when you said that a bus driver is a person (who, whom) tells everyone where to get off?

8. A jury is the only thing that doesn't work right when (it's, they're) fixed!

9. Last year my family and (I, me) visited the Kremlin in the Soviet Union and learned that—in Russian—"Kremlin" means "fortress."

10. In (her or his, their) book on the history of dancing, the teacher and the artist point out that the jitterbug was not an insect but a human being acting like one!

11. Silence, my father told (us, we) girls, may be a successful substitute for lack of brains!

12. According to (whoever, whomever) wrote the story, Margaret Mitchell's novel *Gone With the Wind* has been published in every industrialized country except the Soviet Union.

13. "Gambling," my father said grimly to Mac and (me, myself), "is a procedure whereby you get nothing for something."

14. The elephant, (which, who) is the heaviest of all land animals, walks on its toes.

## PRACTICE SESSION 43 — Mixed Bag

Each of the sentences below contains two (or possibly more) errors. Find them; identify them; correct them.

1. It seems like the hardest people to convince that they're ready to retire is children at bedtime!

2. Being that Thomas Edison is so smart, why didn't he invent a noiseless lawnmower?

3. One reason you can't never take money with you is because it goes before you do!

4. In Japan, neither the two boys nor their sister are enjoying sushi which is a circle of raw fish packed in rice.

5. In regards to your follow-up query of January 12, I wish to state that the only part of this car that don't now make a noise is the horn!

6. George Washington sometimes mispelled words; he often writes "blew" for "blue" and "oyl" for "oil."

7. Could it have been her who made the unforgetable statement that a human body, properly cared for, will last for a lifetime?

8. Everything happens so quick here that one of our foreign visitors insist that an American hour is only forty minutes long!

9. My senior class, accompanied by three chaperons, are going to visit Paros, Greece, where octopi are hanged up to dry alongside towels and sheets.

10. The easiest way to loose control of the car is forgetting to make the payments!

11. A number of people thinks SPUD is an acronym for the Society for Prevention of Unwholesome Diet, an Irish group that believes potatos are poisonous.

12. Jed boasting aggravated me until I remembered that the fellow who blows his horn the loudest is usually in a fog!

13. When she bragged that her ancestors came over on the *Mayflower*, Clever Cal retorted: "Emigration laws are stricter now!"

14. If he dodges cars, hes a pedestrian, if he dodges taxes, he's a millionaire, if he dodges issues, he's a politician.

## PRACTICE SESSION 44 — Verb Roundup

Which word in parentheses is correct? Why?

1. Since three-fourths of the earth's surface (are, is) water and one-fourth is land, we can (imply, infer) that God meant us to spend three times as much time fishing as plowing!

2. In a new magazine, she read that Bob Hope (had been, was) a prize-fighter before he (became, become) a comedian.

3. If Robin Hood (was, were) alive today, he'd steal from the poor because the rich (carries, carry) credit cards!

4. Grandma (sat, set) in her chair and declared that if you give a child an inch, he (shall think, will think) he's a ruler!

5. If there (are, is) twenty-one blue jays on a fence and a hunter shoots six, how many (are, is) left? (Answer: none—the rest would have flown away!)

6. The rest of the astronomers (know, knows) that in Yugoslavia a law was (passed, past) prohibiting Halley's Comet from passing overhead!

7. I was (laying, lying) on the beach, but I (sprang, sprung) up when I heard my mother say I had as much initiative as an echo!

8. This epitaph is (written, wrote) on a New Mexican tombstone: "Here (lays, lies) John Yeast. Pardon me for not rising."

9. Just when I had (learned, taught) myself all life's answers, somebody (began, begun) changing all the questions!

10. Our police department (work, works) on the theory that if burglars are (left, let) alone, they will become rich enough to quit!

11. The doctor (showed, shown) us an article that said mumps (are, is) far more serious for adults than for children.

12. McDonald's (prays, preys) on cows: one out of every ten (end, ends) up in a McDonald hamburger!

13. Do you (accept, except) the idea that there has never been a society in which the majority of the people (was, were) left-handed?

14. Either my sister or her best friend (are, is) responsible for the sign that the drugstore clerk (hanged, hung) on the wall: "Try our cough syrup. You'll never get any better."

*Laugh Your Way Through Grammar*

## PRACTICE SESSION 45 — Rewriting

Transform each of the following dialogue jokes into one or two well-written sentences. Experiment with different patterns, with different types of sentence structure.

---

Example:    Teacher: Why is "b" a hot letter?
            Suzy: Because it makes "oil" "boil"!

Rewrites:   When the teacher asked Suzy why "b" is a hot letter, Suzy quipped: "Because it makes 'oil' 'boil'!"

            Asked by her teacher why "b" is a hot letter, Suzy quickly retorted: "Because it makes 'oil' 'boil'!"

            The teacher asked Suzy why "b" is a hot letter. Suzy thought for a while and then asked timidly: "Because it makes 'oil' 'boil'?"

Or even—    "B" is a hot letter because it makes "oil" "boil"!

---

1.  Kevin:  What kind of bars can't keep convicts in prison?
    Ellie:   Chocolate bars!

2.  Customer:  I'm giving a dinner for all my friends tonight.
    Waiter:     Oh, you must be the gentleman who reserved a table for two!

3.  Teacher: Evelyn, name two pronouns.
    Evelyn:  Who, me?
    Teacher: Correct!

4.  Teacher: What is the plural of "man"?
    Sally:     Men.
    Teacher: And what is the plural of "child"?
    Sally:     Twins!

5.  Teacher: What's the difference between ignorance and apathy?
    Student: I don't know, and I don't care.

6.  Ron:  A bicycle can't stand by itself.
    Don:  Why can't a bicycle stand by itself?
    Ron:  Because it's too (two) tired!

## PRACTICE SESSION 46 — Punctuation Roundup

No punctuation at all has been provided in the following letter. Your task is to provide any punctuation marks needed. You should find about thirty-two.

10 Greenvale Court
Merrydale Ohio 12801
February 25 19_ _

Mr Edward R Lowell Manager
Gleeful Gadgets Inc
17 Forty third Street
New Haven Ohio 12801

Dear Mr Lowell

Some time ago I read about a thermometer ring a gadget invented by Robert Kall in 1982 It is a sort of signet ring with a crystal face that tells its wearer his or her temperature

Since my uncle collects gadgets loves rings and is a bit of a hypochondriac this ring would be a perfect gift for him I do not know whether the ring has ever been manufac tured but if it is available I decided you Mr Lowell are the most likely supplier

Do you have any of these thermometer rings in stock If you dont do you know where I might find one I am really interested in purchasing this interesting gadget if the price is not too high

Very truly yours

Roberta A Black

*Laugh Your Way Through Grammar*

**HOLD IT! The next four Practice Sessions are a little different. Before proceeding, read the directions below.**

1. Read the selection once.

2. Read the selection again, this time with pen in hand.

3. Identify—and correct—all the errors you can find. Blunders may be errors of grammar, of confused words, of punctuation or capitalization, even of spelling.

4. Underline, circle, cross out, delete . . . as shown in the sample paragraph below. If you do not own this book, rewrite each paragraph correctly on a separate sheet of paper.

---

Teddy Roosevelt was ~~quiet~~ *quite* a man. It was ~~him~~ *he* who~~m~~ was the first ꟼresident to ride in an airplane, ꞇhe first to ride in a submarine, *and* ꞇhe first to ride down ᴮbroadway in a tickertape parade. It was ~~him~~ *he*, ~~two~~ *too*, who~~m~~ coined a couple of words: ⟨"pussyfooting" and "mollycoddle." Most astonishing of all, he— alone among UˏˏS, presidents—delivered his inaugural address without once using the ~~personnel~~ *personal* pronoun "I"!

---

NOW IT'S YOUR TURN . . .

## PRACTICE SESSION 47 — Mastery Exercise

One day Jeff told Jean and I about George Willig whom, he said is sometimes known as the "human fly. Once he decided to secretly climb up the outside of the World Trade Center in New York city. In three and a half hours reaching the one hundredth and tenth floor. Since these kind of an activity is frowned upon in the City, Willig was fined one penny for each floor he climbed. A total of $1.10!

## PRACTICE SESSION 48 — Mastery Exercise

No one know exactly when breakfast—as a seperate meal—first started. (*Breakfast*, of course, is the meal at which you *break* your *fast*.) Queen Elizabeth I of england (1533 1603) was a breakfast connoisseur, consuming beef soup goose pie and wheat bread and butter all washed down with beer ale and wine! On this here continent the indians settled for cornmeal mush. Each morning George Washington downed 3 cornmeal hoe-cakes and three cupsful of tea. Thomas Jefferson woke up with chicken cold meats bacon eggs batter cakes fried apples and hot breads. In the last few decades people ofen skipped breakfast completely but now this meal that starts our day are becoming popular again. Many people are dropping in at fast-food eateries for egg and sausage on muffin and having a glass of diet soda—a menu that may suit the modern waistline but that would have been jeered by Elizabeth I and Jefferson!

## PRACTICE SESSION 49 — Mastery Exercise

### The origin of the word "jalopy"

Zach and Zelda was visiting me one Sunday. Zelda said her and her brother just learned why my beat-up car is called a "jalopy."

"Tell me about it," I said, a bit mad.

Zach did most of the telling. "About fifty years ago, alot of old cars—cars like your's Vince—was falling apart, and nobody wanted them. So they begun shipping them off to a small city somewheres in Mexico."

Zelda interrupted. "There they fixed the cars—you know, they repaired them and repainted them until they looked more prettier." "Then what?" I asked.

Zach grinned. "Then they sent it to Mexico City for resale!"

"I still don't get it," I protested. "What does all this have to do with the word "jalopy"?

"The city where the cars were overhauled—what do you think it was named? asked Zach. I shrugged.

Zach and Zelda shouted gleeful, "Jalapa, of course!"

## PRACTICE SESSION 50 — Mastery Exercise

### Pinheads—then and now

At one time if someone called you a "pinhead," you would have become angry with them—but no more. Today the inelegant word identifys not an idiot, but a person whom is a collector of pins especially of Olympic pins.

The Olympic pin started modestly in the early 1900s as an identification badge for game officials. Today some of the most unique pins features Sam the Eagle (mascot of the 1984 L.A. games), polar bears Hidy and Howdy (mascots of the 1988 Calgary games), raccoons on bobsleds, names of favorite competitors, and participating countries put their flags on them. Altogether, at least a quarter of a billion pins all ready circulating throughout the worlds nations.

What does one do with them?

Well if your a sports lover, you pin them proudly to your vest, parka, cap, or towel—even to your christmas stocking! If you're an Olympic athelete, you used them as currency, perhaps leaving one as a tip to a delighted waiter. If you're a tycoon, you buy low, trade, and sell high—ofen at a tremendous profit. (For the moneymaker, there is even pin "stock-market" reports!)

So the next time one of your friends call you a pinhead, chuckle smugly. A Burmese Olympic pin that formally sold for a few dollars is now worth $6,000, at that rate of return, even the most sensitive person shouldn't mind being called a pinhead!

# SECTION II

# The Sentence and Its Parts

53

# 1. THE PARTS OF SPEECH

Words are classified according to how they are used in a sentence to express a thought. All of them fall into eight groups, called the **parts of speech.** A word may be a . . .

| | |
|---|---|
| *noun:* | JIM bought a BOOK about DINOSAURS. |
| *pronoun:* | SHE told HER friends that THEY could accompany HER to Europe. |
| *verb:* | He WALKS to school when he IS happy. |
| *adjective:* | THE BIG, RED apple is BEAUTIFUL. |
| *adverb:* | She ran FAST and was QUICKLY tired. |
| *preposition:* | IN one minute he ran TO the store FOR milk. |
| *conjunction:* | Mary AND Zach are going, BUT Al isn't SINCE he has a previous appointment. |
| *interjection:* | HELP! The boat is sinking! |

The parts of speech are discussed separately in Section III, "The Parts of Speech."

# 2. THE SENTENCE

A **sentence** is a group of words expressing a complete thought.

It may be very short:

Go.

It may be very long:

> Although he had walked for twenty miles along the
> dusty country road, he was neither tired nor bored;
> for he had, with a keen eye, observed the fragile bark
> of a white birch and the fragile wing of a butterfly and
> had, with a keen ear, heard the whirr of the cicada
> and the haunting notes of a pair of loons.

## 3. SUBJECT AND PREDICATE

All the words in a sentence can be divided into two large groups, the *subject* and the *predicate*.

**a. The subject.** The subject is the person, place, thing, or idea about which something is said. The subject may be a **noun** or a **pronoun.**

> *Tom* went to school.
> *She* played hopscotch.
> *Paris* is the capital of France.
> *Justice* prevailed.

**b. The predicate.** The predicate makes a statement about the subject. The chief predicate word is the **verb.**

> Tom *went* . . .
> She *played* . . .
> Paris *is* . . .
> Justice *prevailed* . . .

**c. The simple subject and the simple predicate.** A sentence may be very short. Nevertheless, to be a sentence, a group of words must have a subject and a predicate.

> Students failed.

In this sentence, *students* (a noun) is the **simple subject,** and *failed* (a verb) is the **simple predicate.**

**d. The complete subject and the complete predicate.** If the sentence is enlarged, *students* remains the simple subject and *failed* the simple predicate (or verb).

noun      verb

Several bright students failed an easy test.

*complete subject*      *complete predicate*

## 4. SUBJECT AND VERB (continued)

A sentence contains a *subject* and a *predicate verb* (3).

**a.** The subject may be a **proper noun.**

> *George Washington* was our first president.
> The *Lincoln Memorial* is beautiful.

**b.** The subject may be **"understood"**—not stated. Usually the understood subject is *you*.

> Go to school. (*You* is the understood subject.)

**c.** The subject may be **compound:** that is, made up of two or more subjects connected by a *coordinate conjunction—and, or, but.*

> *Jason* and *Betty* went to the movies.
> The fierce *lion* and the gentle *lamb* are friends.

**d.** The verb may be **"understood"**—not stated.

> Who broke the window? Nan. (*Did* is understood.)

**e.** The verb may consist of more than one word, in which case the verb is called a **verb phrase.** A verb phrase contains the principal verb plus one or more **auxiliary,** or **helping, verbs.** Common helping verbs include the following: be, am, is, are, was, were, been; do, did; will, shall, would, should; may, must, might; can, could; has, have, had.

Eddie *wrote* an essay.   (simple verb)
Eddie *will write* an essay.   (verb phrase)
Eddie *has written* many essays.   (verb phrase)

**f.** The verb may be **compound:** that is, made up of two or more verbs connected by a *coordinate conjunction—and, or, but.*

An elephant cannot *run* or *trot.*

## 5, 6. PHRASES AND CLAUSES

These sentence parts are often confused although they are significantly different. A *phrase* does not have a subject and a predicate (3), but a *clause* does.

**5.** A **phrase** is a group of two or more related words conveying a single thought and not having a subject and a predicate. Kinds of phrases are listed below.

*verb phrase* (4-e):

> Someday some smart guy *will throw* a rubber band into the computer and it *will make* snap decisions!

*infinitive phrase* (48-c):

> Said the mechanic: "My advice is *to keep the oil* and *to change the car.*"

*participial phrase* (49-d):

> *Grinning mischievously,* Larry wrote this brief review of the book he had read: "The covers are too far apart."

*gerund phrase* (50-b):

> *Swallowing angry words* is better than *choking on an apology.*

*prepositional phrase* (65):

> An obstetrician may be defined as someone who makes all her
> money *on the stork market*.

**6.** A **clause** is a group of related words having a subject and a predicate.
There are two kinds of clauses: the *independent* (or *main*) clause and
the *dependent* (or *subordinate*) clause.

$$\underset{\text{independent clause}}{\underline{\overset{s \qquad v}{\text{Everyone applauded the mayor}}}} \quad \underset{\text{dependent clause}}{\underline{\overset{s \qquad v}{\text{when he promised a bike lane.}}}}$$

$$\underset{\text{dependent clause}}{\underline{\overset{s \qquad v}{\text{Because the roads were icy,}}}} \quad \underset{\text{independent clause}}{\underline{\overset{s \qquad v}{\text{the Smiths canceled their visit.}}}}$$

**a.** An **independent clause** has a subject and a predicate and expresses a complete thought. In the above sentences, the subject (*s*)
and the verb (*v*) of each clause are indicated.

**b.** A **dependent clause** cannot stand alone as a sentence. Although
containing a subject and a verb, it does not express a complete thought.

$$\overset{s \qquad v}{\text{when he promised a bike lane}}$$

$$\overset{s \qquad v}{\text{Because the roads were icy}}$$

**c.** Some dependent clauses begin with a *subordinate conjunction* (72-
b). *When*, *because*, and *although* are common subordinate conjunctions. A subordinate conjunction joins the dependent clause with the
independent clause.

dependent:   although the pitcher threw a fast curve
independent:  the boy hit the ball

joined:   Although the pitcher threw a fast curve, the boy
        hit the ball.
or:   The boy hit the ball although the pitcher threw
        a fast curve.

Another example:

> dependent: when I arrived at the station
> independent: the train had already left
>
> joined: When I arrived at the station, the train had already left.
> or: The train had already left when I arrived at the station.

**d.** Some dependent clauses begin with a *relative pronoun* (30). A relative pronoun functions like a subordinate conjunction: it joins the dependent clause with the independent clause to form a complete complex sentence.

> dependent: that Jess requested
> independent: here is the book
> joined: Here is the book that Jess requested.
>
> dependent: who is my sister
> independent: Cecilia is a karate expert
> joined: Cecilia, who is my sister, is a karate expert.

**e.** Dependent clauses are used in different ways.

(1) **AS A NOUN** (answers the question "what" or "who")

*noun clause used as subject of a sentence* (3-a):

> *That she is brilliant* is obvious.
> *Where he studied medieval history* is uncertain.
> (Notice that a noun clause, however it is used, answers the question "what" or "who.")

*noun clause used as a predicate noun* (7-f ):

> This is *what I require.*
> The reason she is ill is *that she doesn't eat properly.*

*noun clause used as the direct object* (7-b):

> Suddenly he remembered *where he had left his bicycle.*
> He feared *that his mother would scold him.*

*noun clause used as object of a preposition* (64-b):

> A prize will be given to *whoever wins the contest.*
> Pack your suitcase with *whatever you wish to take with you.*

*noun clause used as an appositive* (17, 18):

> The decision *that Mary should be our representative* pleased
> everyone.
> We have every hope *that he will rescue us.*

*noun clause used as the subject of a sentence beginning with "it"*

> It is essential *that you attend the conference.*
>> (The noun clause is the true subject of *is*; "it" is
>> merely an introductory word, an expletive. In subject-
>> verb order, the sentence would read. *That you attend
>> the conference* is essential.)

> (2) **AS AN ADJECTIVE** (answers the question
> "which one" or "what kind of")

*adjective clause modifying a noun or pronoun* (30):

> The boat *that won the race* belongs to my uncle.
> Ellie is the candidate *whom I prefer.*
>> (Notice that an adjective clause, like an adjective, an-
>> swers the question "which one" or "what kind of.")

> (3) **AS AN ADVERB** (answers the question
> "where," "when," "why," "how," or "to
> what degree")

*adverb clause modifying a verb, adjective, or another adverb* (57, 58):

> I will clean the house *while you are shopping.*
> Listen carefully *so that you will be able to answer my questions.*
>> (Notice that an adverb clause, like an adverb, answers the question "where," "when," "why," "how," or "to what degree.")

## 7. COMPLEMENTS

**a.** As said before, some sentences are complete with only a subject and a verb as its main parts. Examples: "Harry fell." "Several children cried." "The plane landed safely." But some sentences require a third part, a complement. A **complement** is a word that completes the meaning of a verb.

Each sentence illustrated below has a subject and a verb, but the verb does not make a complete statement about the subject . . . until a complement (capitalized) is added.

> For dinner, I had . . . a juicy STEAK.
>> (direct object)

> We sent . . . ANITA . . . a Barbie DOLL.
>> (indirect object and direct object)

> The winner of the rodeo was . . . ISRAEL.
>> (predicate noun)

> Helen is always . . . CHEERFUL.
>> (predicate adjective)

**b.** The **direct object** is the person, place, thing, or idea that receives the action. It answers the question *what* or *whom*.

> The juniors decorated the *gym.*
>> *d.o.*

> Eleanor called *me* yesterday.
>> *d.o.*

**c.** The **indirect object** is the person or thing "to whom" something is given or "for whom" something is done. It always precedes the direct object.

> Eleanor pitched *him* a strike.
>          *i.o.*     *d.o.*
>
> Juan told his little *sister* a story.
>         *i.o.*     *d.o.*
>
> Make Alicia a hamburger.
>    *i.o.*     *d.o.*

**d.** An object (direct or indirect) may be a *noun*, a *pronoun*, or a *verbal*.

> Liz called *Michael*. (a noun)
> Liz called *him*. (a pronoun)
> Liz enjoys *swimming*. (a verbal: gerund)
> Liz likes *to swim*. (a verbal: infinitive)

**e.** A **compound object** (whether direct or indirect) is made up of two or more objects connected by a *coordinate conjunction—and, or, but*.

> Alison carried a *blanket* and a *thermos* to the game.
>           *d.o.*          *d.o.*
> (compound direct object)

> Their mother gave *Norma* and *Norman* some spaghetti.
>           *i.o.*     *i.o.*    *d.o.*
> (compound indirect object)

**f.** A *noun, pronoun,* or *adjective* after a **linking verb** (44) redefines or describes the subject. They lie in the predicate but refer to the subject. (See 3, subject and predicate.)

> Jim is an *actor*. (predicate noun)
> *s*

> It is *I*. (predicate pronoun)
> *s*

> Small children are often *creative*. (predicate adjective)
> *s*

## 8. MODIFIERS

**a.** A **modifier** is a word that tells something about another word. By providing a specific detail, a modifier *describes* or *limits* the meaning of the modified word.

> She is an *intelligent* girl.
> (tells a *characteristic* of the girl)

> Elsie painted a *red* schoolhouse.
> (tells the *color* of the schoolhouse)

> In baseball, *nine* men take the field.
> (tells the *number* of players)

> *That* fellow is my brother.
> (tells *which one*)

> Ms. Brown selected *Isidore's* composition.
> (tells *whose*)

**b.** Adjectives and adverbs are modifiers. The italicized modifiers in the sentences above are **adjectives** (52). They tell something about *nouns* or *pronouns*.

Other modifiers, italicized below, are **adverbs** (57). They tell something about *verbs* in the following sentences.

> We will leave for the airport *soon*.
> (tells *when*)

> After school I went *home*.
> (tells *where*; see also 59-b)

> I answered *thoughtfully*.
> (tells *how*; *in what manner*)

> She practices *daily*.
> (tells *how often*)

**c.** Adjectives and adverbs are classified according to *how they are used in sentences*.

(1)  An adjective modifies a noun or pronoun.

> The *pretty* girl won the contest.
>
>> (modifies the noun *girl*)
>
> She is *pretty*.
>
>> (modifies the pronoun *she*; see predicate adjective, 7-f.)

(2)  An adverb, most commonly, modifies a verb (57), but it may also modify an adjective or another adverb (58).

> Ron *quickly* sliced the cucumber.
>
>> (modifies the verb *sliced*)
>
> Ron is *disturbingly* clever.
>
>> (modifies the predicate adjective *clever*)
>
> Ron spoke *almost* brilliantly about skin diving.
>
>> (modifies the adverb *brilliantly*)

## 9. TYPES OF SENTENCES

We classify sentences in two ways:

(1)  by the way we EXPRESS thoughts (10):

(declarative, interrogative, imperative, exclamatory)

(2)  by the way we STRUCTURE sentences to convey these thoughts (11):

(simple, compound, complex, compound-complex)

## 10. DECLARATIVE, INTERROGATIVE, IMPERATIVE, AND EXCLAMATORY SENTENCES

These are the four types of sentences by which we **express** our thoughts: (*a*) the *declarative*, (*b*) the *interrogative*, (*c*) the *imperative*, and (*d*) the *exclamatory*.

**a.** The **declarative sentence** makes a statement. It ends with a period.

> Candy is sweet**.**

**b.** The **interrogative sentence** asks a question. It ends with a question mark.

> Do you like candy**?**

**c.** The **imperative sentence** gives a command. It ends with a period.

> Beware of the dog**.**
> Do your homework now**.**

**d.** The **exclamatory sentence** expresses strong emotion. It ends with an exclamation point. It may be composed of only one word: an *interjection* (76); or it may be composed of several words.

> Help**!**
> The building is on fire**!**

## 11. SIMPLE, COMPOUND, COMPLEX, AND COMPOUND-COMPLEX SENTENCES

These are the four types of sentences according to **structure:** (*a*) the *simple*, (*b*) the *compound*, (*c*) the *complex*, and (*d*) the *compound-complex*.

*Laugh Your Way Through Grammar*

**a.** The **simple sentence** consists of one independent clause (6-a). It has one subject and one predicate although either (or both) may be **compound.**

> Archie <u>played</u> football.
>
>> (simple sentence: simple subject and simple predicate)
>
> <u>Archie</u> and <u>Marilyn</u> <u>played</u> football.
>
>> (simple sentence: compound subject and simple predicate)
>
> <u>Archie</u> and <u>Marilyn</u> <u>played</u> football and <u>wrote</u> stories.
>
>> (simple sentence: compound subject and compound predicate)

Note: It would be a mistake to say that, in sentence 3, *Archie* and *Marilyn* are two subjects, or that *played* and *wrote* are two predicates.

**b.** The **compound sentence** consists of two or more independent clauses connected by a coordinate conjunction. A **comma** is usually placed before the coordinate conjunction in a compound sentence. (The independent clauses are underlined.)

> <u>Dan knew all about fishing</u>, *but* <u>his little brother caught the big one.</u>
>
> <u>An optimist laughs to forget</u>, *but* <u>a pessimist forgets to laugh.</u>

## Punctuation Aids

(1) Use a comma followed by a coordinate conjunction to separate the independent clauses.

> Archie played football, *and* Marilyn wrote stories.

(2) Or, use a semicolon (without a comma and without a conjunction) to separate the clauses.

> Archie played football; Marilyn wrote stories.

**c.** The **complex sentence** consists of one independent clause and one or more dependent clauses (6-b). (The dependent clauses in the examples below are underlined.)

> After she had finished shopping, Nell went to wrestling practice.
>
>> ("After she had finished shopping" is a dependent clause: it cannot stand alone. "Nell went to wrestling practice" is the independent clause.)

> I never knew what a poor loser I was until I went on a diet!
>
>> ("What a poor loser I was" is a dependent clause; so is "until I went on a diet." "I never knew" is the independent clause.)

**Punctuation Aids**

(1) If a *dependent* clause begins a sentence, a comma follows the clause.

> After they had dinner, they went to the theater.

(2) If an *independent* clause begins a sentence, usually no comma follows it.

> They went to the theater after they had dinner.

(3) If a *dependent* clause is located in the middle of a sentence, the clause is usually preceded and followed by a comma.

> My friends, after they had dinner, went to the theater.

**d.** The **compound-complex sentence** consists of two or more independent clauses and one or more dependent clauses. (The independent clauses in each example below are underlined.)

> If he tries, I will help Jim write his essay, but I will not write it for him.
>
>> ("If he tries" is a dependent clause; "I . . . essay" and "I . . . him" are independent clauses.)

<u>Keep a ruler on the newspaper</u> as you read it, and <u>you'll get the story straight!</u>

> ("As . . . it" is a dependent clause; "Keep . . . newspaper" and "you'll . . . straight" are independent clauses.)

## 12-16. COMMON SENTENCE STRUCTURE ERRORS

**12.** Sentence fragment. A sentence that is not complete in itself is called a **sentence fragment:** (SF). The sentence may lack (*a*) a *subject*, (*b*) a *predicate*, or (*c*) *both a subject and a predicate.*

**a.** Wrong: Sent me a bouquet of roses on my birthday.
  (Add a subject.)
  Right: *My brother* sent me a bouquet of roses on my birthday.

**b.** Wrong: Bobby having a fine scrimshaw collection.
  (Change *having* to a predicate verb.)
  Right: Bobby *has* a fine scrimshaw collection.

**c.** Wrong: After the game was over and everyone had gone home.
  (Add a subject and a predicate to the dependent clause.)
  Right: After the game was over and everyone had gone home, *the custodians cleared the field.*

A fragment may also be (*d*) a *phrase*, (*e*) a *clause*, or (*f*) a *series of words incorrectly written as if it were a sentence.* As shown below, the fragment should be attached to the main clause.

**d.** Wrong: Eternity is paying for a car. <u>On the installment plan.</u>
  (Attach the prepositional phrase to the main clause.)
  Right: Eternity is paying for a car *on the installment plan.*

**e.** Wrong: Football is the cleanest of all sports. <u>Because it's the only one with scrub teams.</u>
  (Attach the subordinate clause to the main clause.)
  Right: Football is the cleanest of all sports *because it's the only one with scrub teams.*

**f.** Wrong: Love is a word made up of two consonants and two vowels. <u>And two fools.</u>
(Attach the fragment to the main clause.)

Right: Love is a word made up of two consonants and two vowels—*and two fools*.

**13.** Run-on Sentence. When two sentences are run together without a coordinate conjunction to link the clauses or without a semicolon to separate them, the result is called a **run-on sentence:** ROS.

Wrong: Lazy Lou heard that a particular machine would do half
his work he ordered two!

To correct a run-on sentence, try one of these procedures.

**a.** Form two sentences. End the first sentence with a period followed
by a capital letter.

Right: Lazy Lou heard that a particular machine would do half
his work. **H**e ordered two!

**b.** Or form a compound sentence (11-b). Link the clauses with a
comma and a coordinate conjunction.

Right: Lazy Lou heard that a particular machine would do half
his work, **and** he ordered two!

**c.** Or form a compound sentence by connecting the clauses with a
semicolon.

Right: Lazy Lou heard that a particular machine would do half
his work; he ordered two!

**d.** Or form a complex sentence (11-c). Study the Punctuation Aids
in 11-c.

Right: When Lazy Lou heard that a particular machine would do
half his work, he ordered two!

**14.** Comma fault. When two sentences are connected by a comma, the result is a **comma fault sentence:** CF.

> Wrong: Golf was once a rich man's sport, now it has millions of poor players.

To correct a comma fault sentence, follow the same procedures as those for correcting run-on sentences (13).

**a.** Form two sentences. End the first sentence with a period followed by a capital letter.

> Right:　Golf was once a rich man's sport. **Now** it has millions of poor players.

**b.** Or form a compound sentence (11-b). Link the clauses with a comma and a coordinate conjunction.

> Right:　Golf was once a rich man's sport, **but** now it has millions of poor players.

**c.** Or form a compound sentence by connecting the clauses with a semicolon.

> Right:　Golf was once a rich man's sport; now it has millions of poor players.

**d.** Or form a complex sentence (11-c). Study the Punctuation Aids in 11-c.

> Right:　Although golf was once a rich man's sport, now it has millions of poor players.

**15.** Misplaced modifier. When a modifier is placed incorrectly, a **misplaced modifier** occurs. A modifier should be placed as close as possible to the word it modifies.

*The Sentence and Its Parts*

**a.** The position of the modifier should be decided on the basis of logic.

(1) Wrong:  Amy selected a dress *in the store* that was made of red silk.

> (Was the store made of red silk? Place the phrase "in the store" at the beginning of the sentence so that "dress" and the clause that describes the dress appear together.)

Right:  *In the store* Amy selected a dress that was made of red silk.

(2) Wrong:  We saw a child in the car *wearing a bunny suit.*

> (The car was wearing a bunny suit? Place the phrase "wearing a bunny suit" next to *child*, the noun that the phrase modifies.)

Right:  We saw a child *wearing a bunny suit* in the car.

(3) Wrong:  Felix spotted the fire *walking down the street.*

> (A fire can walk? Place the phrase "walking down the street" at the beginning of the sentence, next to the noun *Felix*, which the phrase modifies.)

Right:  *Walking down the street*, Felix spotted the fire.

**b.** If one noun has a modifier and the other doesn't, place the noun with the modifier second.

(4) Wrong:  He enjoys *downhill skiing* and *skating.*

> (Is the skating downhill?)

Right:  He enjoys *skating* and *downhill skiing.*

**c.** Sometimes moving a misplaced modifier is not enough. It may be necessary to rewrite the sentence or even to create two sentences.

(5) Wrong:  Wearing riding boots and safari jackets, the two dogs accompanied their adventurous owners.

> (Were the dogs so clad? Rewrite the sentence.)

Right:  The two dogs accompanied their adventurous owners, who were wearing riding boots and safari jackets.

**16.** Dangling modifier. When there is nothing in a sentence for a modifier to refer to, a **dangling modifier** occurs.

Wrong: Speeding around the corner, a child was hit.

> (WHO was speeding around the corner?)

Right: Speeding around the corner, the *car* hit a child.

Wrong: The closet is to the right on entering.

> (WHO is entering?)

Right: The closet is to the right as *you* enter.

or: On entering, *you* will find the closet is to the right.

Wrong: Strolling down the street, the Washington Monument was a magnificent sight.

> (WHO was strolling?)

Right: Strolling down the street, *we* found the Washington Monument a magnificent sight.

or: As *we* strolled down the street, the Washington Monument was a magnificent sight.

## 17-20. VARIATIONS IN SENTENCE STRUCTURE

## THE APPOSITIVE

**17.** An **appositive** is a word, phrase, or clause that tells something about a preceding noun. The appositive explains the noun: (*a*) *defines* it, (*b*) *describes* it, or (*c*) *identifies* it.

**a.** Jess enjoys using the word gargalesthesia, *the sensation that you get when you're tickled.*

> ("The sensation . . . tickled" is an appositive, defining *gargalesthesia.*)

**b.** The mongoose, *a black or brown animal with a long tail*, is being trained to detect drugs at the international airport in Sri Lanka.

> ("A black . . . tail" is an appositive, describing *mongoose.*)

**c.** The zoo acquired a boomer, *a male kangaroo*, and a flier, *a female kangaroo*.

("A male kangaroo" is an appositive, identifying *boomer*; and "a female kangaroo" is an appositive, identifying *flier*.)

**18.** A word, phrase, or clause may be in apposition with (*a*) a *subject*, (*b*) a *direct object* (7-b), (*c*) an *indirect object* (7-c), (*d*) or a *predicate noun* (7-f).

**a.** In 1787, Alexander Hamilton, *the Revolutionary statesman*, described the Constitution as "a shilly-shally thing of milk and water, which could not last."

(in apposition with the subject, *Alexander Hamilton*)

**b.** Emily operates a "bawlroom," *a nursery for small children*.

(in apposition with the direct object, *bawlroom*)

**c.** The doctor gave Emily, *my best friend*, some good news.

(in apposition with the indirect object, *Emily*)

**d.** Millie is an egoist, *someone who suffers from "I" strain*.

(in apposition with the predicate noun, *egoist*)

## 19. PUNCTUATION AIDS

**a.** If an appositive ends a sentence, it is usually separated from the rest of the sentence by a comma.

In an emergency he always calls Jeremy, *his big brother*.

**b.** If an appositive is within a sentence, it is usually separated by two commas from the rest of the sentence.

Jeremy, *his big brother*, is always available in an emergency.

## PARALLEL STRUCTURE

**20.** Parallel structure requires that parallel thoughts be expressed in similar (or parallel) grammatical terms.

**a.** *Independent Clauses* (6-a):

> Wrong: I washed the dishes, I dried the dishes, and as for putting them away, I did that, too.
>
> Right: *I washed the dishes, I dried the dishes*, and *I put the dishes away.*

**b.** *Dependent Clauses* (6-b):

> Wrong: I promised Mr. Smith that Ellie would wash the car, the waxing would be done by Jim, and the necessary touch-up work by me.
>
> Right: I promised Mr. Smith *that Ellie would wash the car, that Jim would wax it*, and *that I'd do the necessary touch-up work.*

**c.** *Nouns* (22):

> Wrong: Jason has big muscles and is very strong.
>
> Right: Jason has big *muscles* and great *strength.*

> Wrong: Lori bought tomatoes, cucumbers, and something to snack on.
>
> Right: Lori bought *tomatoes, cucumbers*, and *snacks.*

**d.** *Pronouns* (37-e): (unnecessary shift in pronoun)

> Wrong: If one studies, you can pass the test.
>
> Right: If *one* studies, *one* can pass the test.
>
> or: If *you* study, *you* can pass the test.

**e.** *Verbs* (40-a): (unnecessary shift in tense)

Wrong: Pat shook his head, frowned, and moves away.
Right: Pat *shook* his head, *frowned*, and *moved* away.
or: Pat *shakes* his head, *frowns*, and *moves* away.

Wrong: She walked to the store and buys a quart of milk.
Right: She *walks* to the store and *buys* a quart of milk.
or: She *walked* to the store and *bought* a quart of milk.

**f.** *Verbs* (45-c): (unnecessary shift in voice)

Wrong: Jack did secretarial work, Jill did accounting, and nothing was done by Sally.
Right: *Jack did* secretarial work, *Jill did* accounting, and *Sally did* nothing.

**g.** *Infinitives* (48-a):

Wrong: He likes to swim, go boating, and surfing.
Right: He likes *to swim*, *to boat*, and *to surf*.
or: He likes *to swim*, *boat*, and *surf*.

**h.** *Gerunds* (50-a):

Wrong: He likes swimming and to go boating and surfing.
Right: He likes *swimming*, *boating*, and *surfing*.

**i.** *Adjectives* (52):

Wrong: Merrilee is tall and has strength.
Right: Merrilee is *tall* and *strong*.

**j.** *Prepositional Phrases* (65):

Wrong: Gertrude, a little kangaroo, is a trademark used in some paperbacks and advertisements.
Right: Gertrude, a little kangaroo, is a trademark used *in some paperbacks* and *in some advertisements*.

**k.** *Correlatives* (certain coordinating conjunctions) (73): Notice that the grammatical construction after EACH conjunction is parallel.

> Wrong: He gave gifts BOTH to his hostess AND her sister.
> Right:  He gave gifts BOTH *to his hostess* AND *to her sister*.

> Wrong: This money is EITHER for you OR your sister.
> Right:  This money is EITHER *for you* OR *for your sister*.
> or:     This money is for EITHER *you* OR *your sister*.

**l.** *Incomplete Parallel Structure:* Be sure to include all the words necessary to make parallel structure complete. An omission can cause incomplete parallel structure *and* make the meaning unclear.

> Wrong: Compare the books in the study with the garage. (Compare "books" with "garage"? Surely not!)
> Right:  Compare the books *in the study* with those *in the garage*.

> Wrong: Dogs chase cats more often than people.
> Right:  *Dogs chase cats* more often than *they chase people*.
> or:     *Dogs chase cats* more often than *people do*.

## 21. SENTENCE COMBINING: A SUMMARY OF SENTENCE STRUCTURE VARIATIONS

**Sentence combining** can turn two or three short, choppy sentences into one smooth, rhythmical sentence. There are a number of procedures for doing this.

**a.** Combine by constructing an APPOSITIVE (17) within a simple sentence.

> Choppy: Clara Barton founded the American Red Cross. At one time, she wanted to be a soldier.
> Smooth: Clara Barton, *the founder of the American Red Cross*, at one time wanted to be a soldier.

**b.** Combine by constructing a PREPOSITIONAL PHRASE (65) within a simple sentence.

> Choppy: Lee went to the store. He wanted to buy two video-tapes and a tape eraser.
> Smooth: Lee went to the store *for two videotapes* and *a tape eraser.*

**c.** Combine by constructing an INFINITIVE PHRASE (48-c) within a simple sentence.

> Choppy: Lee went to the store. He wanted to buy two video-tapes and a tape eraser.
> Smooth: Lee went to the store *to buy two videotapes and a tape eraser.*

**d.** Combine by constructing a PARTICIPIAL PHRASE (49-d) within a simple sentence.

> Choppy: Tim set off for a day of hiking. He was whistling merrily.
> Smooth: *Whistling merrily,* Tim set off for a day of hiking.

**e.** Combine by constructing a COMPOUND SUBJECT (4-c), using a coordinate conjunction to join the subjects.

> Choppy: Human beings flirt. Birds flirt, too.
> Smooth: *Human beings* AND *birds* flirt.

> Choppy: At birth, baby chicks recognize the silhouette of a hawk. So do ducklings. So do goslings.
> Smooth: At birth, *baby chicks*, *ducklings*, AND *goslings* recognize the silhouette of a hawk.

**f.** Combine by constructing a COMPOUND VERB (4-f), using a coordinate conjunction to join the verbs.

> Choppy: Zoo animals that need a vacation slink into hideaways. They sulk.
> Smooth: Zoo animals that need a vacation *slink* into hideaways AND *sulk*.

> Choppy: Two alligators preparing to mate touch each other. They caress each other. They nuzzle each other about the head and neck.
> Smooth: Two alligators preparing to mate *touch*, *caress*, AND *nuzzle* each other about the head and neck.

**g.** Combine by constructing a COMPOUND OBJECT (7-e), using a coordinate conjunction to join the objects.

> Choppy: In a poll, British children said they disliked snakes. They also disliked spiders.
> Smooth: In a poll, British children said they disliked *snakes* AND *spiders*. (compound direct object)

> Choppy: Aaron told me that Henry II (1154–1189) was the first English king to read a book in bed. He told my brother, too.
> Smooth: Aaron told my *brother* AND *me* that Henry II (1154–1189) was the first English king to read a book in bed. (compound indirect object)

**h.** Combine by constructing a COMPOUND SENTENCE (11-b), using a coordinate conjunction or a semicolon (222-a) to join the clauses.

> Choppy: We make a living by what we get. We make a life by what we give.
> Smooth: We make a living by what we get, BUT we make a life by what we give.
> Smooth: We make a living by what we get; we make a life by what we give.

**i.** Combine by constructing a COMPLEX SENTENCE (11-c), using a subordinate conjunction to form a dependent clause.

> Choppy: The tramp asked for something to eat. The farmer suggested that he go to the woodshed and take a few chops.
>
> Smooth: *When the tramp asked for something to eat,* the farmer suggested that he go to the woodshed and take a few chops.

**j.** Combine by constructing a COMPOUND-COMPLEX SENTENCE (11-d).

> Choppy: Corinne is an intelligent girl. She is studying hard. She hopes to win the scholarship.
>
> > First, construct a compound sentence (21-h).
>
> Smooth: Corinne is an intelligent girl, AND she is studying hard.
>
> > Then use a subordinate conjunction to form a dependent clause, and attach the dependent clause to the compound sentence.
>
> Smooth: Corinne is an intelligent girl, AND she is studying hard BECAUSE she hopes to win the scholarship.

**k.** Combine by using PARALLEL STRUCTURE (20).

> Choppy: George likes cats. He also likes dogs. He likes hamsters, too.
>
> Smooth: George likes cats, dogs, and hamsters.

> Choppy: Georgina hits home runs. She throws spectacular passes. She putts with deadly accuracy.
>
> Smooth: Georgina hits home runs, throws spectacular passes, and putts with deadly accuracy.

> Choppy: He told her that she should go to Bermuda. He said she should have a good time. She shouldn't come back, he said, until she was fully rested.
>
> Smooth: He told her that she should go to Bermuda, have a good time, and come back only when she was fully rested.

# SECTION III

# The Parts of Speech

## NOUNS

---

*Continued on Following Page*

# ADJECTIVES

# ADVERBS

# PREPOSITIONS

# CONJUNCTIONS

# INTERJECTIONS

# NOUNS

## 22. A NAME WORD: THE NOUN

A **noun** is the name of a person, place, thing, or event. All nouns are classified as either (*a*) *common* or (*b*) *proper*.

**a.** A **common noun** names *any one* of a class or group of persons, places, things, or events. A **proper noun** names a *particular* person, place, thing, or event.

|  | COMMON NOUN | PROPER NOUN |
|---|---|---|
| *person:* | boy | Tom |
| *place:* | state | Nebraska |
| *thing:* | car | Ford |
| *event:* | war | Revolutionary War |

**b.** A common noun is never capitalized; a proper noun is always capitalized. (For a further study of the capitalization of proper nouns, see 210.)

| NOT CAPITALIZED | CAPITALIZED |
|---|---|
| boy | **T**om **B**rown |
| canyon | **G**rand **C**anyon |
| street | **F**irst **S**treet |

**c.** A **compound noun** is made up of two or more words.

| | |
|---|---|
| mother-in-law | Miami Beach |
| firefighter | Washington, D.C. |
| commander in chief | Secretary of State |

**d.** A **collective noun** names a group.

| | | |
|---|---|---|
| team | class | army |
| audience | jury | committee |

## 23. SINGULAR AND PLURAL OF NOUNS

A noun may be **singular** (*one*) or **plural** (*more than one*) in number. (In grammar, *number* means the form of a word to show whether one or more than one is meant.) To form the plural of most nouns, just add an **s**.

| | |
|---|---|
| dog—dog**s** | house—house**s** |
| toy—toy**s** | tray—tray**s** |

**a.** If a singular noun ends in **ch**, **sh**, **s**, **x**, or **z**, add **es**.

| | |
|---|---|
| church—church**es** | box—box**es** |
| bush—bush**es** | topaz—topaz**es** |
| guess—guess**es** | |

**b.** If a singular noun ends in **y** and the **y** is preceded by a consonant, change the **y** to **i** and add **es**.

| | |
|---|---|
| baby—bab**ies** | fly—fl**ies** |
| lady—lad**ies** | sky—sk**ies** |

However, do *not* follow this rule with proper nouns. You may talk about three "Mar**ys**" or the "Kell**ys**."

**c.** If a singular noun ends in **y** and the **y** is preceded by a vowel, keep the **y** and add **s**. (The *vowels* are *a, e, i, o, u.* All the other letters of the alphabet are *consonants.*)

| | |
|---|---|
| jockey—jockey**s** | turkey—turkey**s** |
| monkey—monkey**s** | day—day**s** |

**d.** If a singular noun ends in **o** and the **o** is preceded by a vowel, add **s**.

| | |
|---|---|
| radio—radio**s** | curio—curio**s** |
| trio—trio**s** | patio—patio**s** |

**e.** If a singular noun ends in **o** and the **o** is preceded by a consonant, add **es**.

| | |
|---|---|
| tomato—tomato**es** | potato—potato**es** |
| hero—hero**es** | veto—veto**es** |

Exceptions: solo**s**; soprano**s**; piano**s**. (usually musical terms)

**f.** If a singular noun ends in **f** or **fe**, sometimes, to form the plural, change the **f** or **fe** to **v** and add **es**.

| | |
|---|---|
| elf—el**ves** | self—sel**ves** |
| half—hal**ves** | sheaf—shea**ves** |
| hoof—hoo**ves** | shelf—shel**ves** |
| knife—kni**ves** | thief—thie**ves** |
| leaf—lea**ves** | wharf—whar**ves** |
| life—li**ves** | wife—wi**ves** |
| loaf—loa**ves** | wolf—wol**ves** |

However, other **f** and **fe** words form the plural by simply adding **s**.

| | |
|---|---|
| belief—belief**s** | gulf—gulf**s** |
| chief—chief**s** | proof—proof**s** |
| cliff—cliff**s** | roof—roof**s** |
| grief—grief**s** | safe—safe**s** |

(One way to be sure of the correct spelling of **f** and **fe** words is to memorize them! Another way is to consult a dictionary.)

**g.** Some nouns form the plural by adding **en** or **ren**.

| | |
|---|---|
| child—child**ren** | ox—ox**en** |

**h.** Some nouns form the plural by changing, adding, or deleting a vowel within the word.

| | |
|---|---|
| man—**men** | woman—**women** |
| mouse—**mice** | goose—**geese** |
| louse—**lice** | tooth—**teeth** |

**i.** Some nouns have the same form, regardless of number.

|              |               |
|--------------|---------------|
| deer—deer    | sheep—sheep   |
| series—series| moose—moose   |

**j.** Some nouns look plural but are actually singular.

|          |           |
|----------|-----------|
| measles  | ethics    |
| mumps    | economics |

Right: *Economics is* a required course in our school.

**k.** Some nouns are always plural, never singular.

|          |          |
|----------|----------|
| trousers | scissors |
| tongs    | clothes  |

**l.** Compound words usually form the plural by adding **s** to the main part of the word.

| mother-in-law     | mother**s**-in-law     |
|-------------------|------------------------|
| Board of Education| Board**s** of Education|
| passerby          | passer**s**by          |

**m.** A singular noun ending in **ful** forms the plural by adding **s** at the end of the word.

| spoonful | spoonful**s** |
|----------|---------------|
| cupful   | cupful**s**   |

**n.** Letters, numbers, and occasionally words form the plural by adding **'s**.

There are three ''2's'' in the example.
There are two ''n's'' in the word ''dinner.''

**o.** A noun borrowed from a foreign language often retains its foreign plural.

| SINGULAR | PLURAL |
|---|---|
| datum | data |
| phenomenon | phenomena |
| alumna | alumnae |
| alumnus | alumni |

## 24. POSSESSIVE CASE OF NOUNS

The **possessive case** is used to show *ownership* or *possession*.

**a. Singular possession:** If a singular noun does not end in **s**, add an apostrophe and **s** (**'s**).

| SINGULAR NOUN | POSSESSIVE CASE |
|---|---|
| Mary | Mary**'s** coat |
| girl | girl**'s** essay |
| clown | clown**'s** painted face |
| giraffe | giraffe**'s** neck |
| book | book**'s** cover |

**b.** If the singular form of a noun ends in **s**, add only an apostrophe instead of **'s** to avoid the awkwardness of the additional **s** sound.

| | |
|---|---|
| Jesus | for Jesus' sake |
| class | our class' record |

**c. Plural possession:** The above rules also apply for forming the possessive case of plural nouns. Hint: first write the plural form of the noun. If the plural noun does not end in **s**, add **'s**.

| PLURAL NOUN | POSSESSIVE CASE |
|---|---|
| men | men**'s** clothing |
| women | women**'s** movement |
| children | children**'s** toys |

**d.** If the plural noun ends in **s**, add only an apostrophe.

| | |
|---|---|
| boys | boys' coats |
| girls | girls' boots |
| officers | officers' orders |

**e.** A compound noun forms the possessive by adding an apostrophe or an **'s** to the last word.

| SINGULAR NOUN | POSSESSIVE CASE |
|---|---|
| sister-in-law | sister-in-law**'s** house |
| Secretary of State | Secretary of State**'s** message |
| United Nations | United Nations' policy |

**f.** If two nouns own the same thing, the apostrophe or **'s** is added to the second noun.

Tom and Dick**'s** dog (both own the same dog)

If each noun owns something individually, the sign of possession is placed after each noun.

Tom**'s** and Dick**'s** feet (each boy has his own feet)

**g.** If a noun precedes a gerund (a verbal noun ending in *ing*), the noun is usually in the possessive case.

The audience applauded David**'s** singing of the national anthem.

# PRONOUNS

## 25. A NOUN SUBSTITUTE: THE PRONOUN

**a.** A **pronoun** is a word that takes the place of a *noun*. By substituting a pronoun for a repeated noun, you produce a smoother sentence.

> Awkward: Tim's very orderly. *Tim* even eats *Tim's* alphabet soup alphabetically!
> Smooth: Tim's very orderly. *He* even eats *his* alphabet soup alphabetically!

> Awkward: Writers are the strangest people: *writers'* tales come out of *writers'* heads!
> Smooth: Writers are the strangest people: *their* tales come out of *their* heads!

**b.** Pronouns cause trouble because they change their form according to how they are used in sentences. For example, *I* changes to *me* and *my* in the following sentences.

> *I* called Frank.
> Frank visited *me*.
> He is *my* cousin.

**c.** The study of pronouns is further complicated by the large number of pronouns in our language and the many groups into which they have been classified.

> personal pronouns (26)
> compound personal pronouns (27)
> demonstrative pronouns (28)
> indefinite pronouns (29)
> relative pronouns (30)
> interrogative pronouns (31)

## 26–31. KINDS OF PRONOUNS

26. **Personal pronouns** refer to *persons*. Certain personal pronouns distinguish the speaker (first person), or the person spoken to (second person), or the person, place, or thing spoken about (third person).

> **First person:** I, my, mine, me, we, our, ours, us
>
> **Second person:** you, your, yours
>
> **Third person:** he, she, it, his, her, hers, its, him, they, their, theirs, them
>
> Note: *it (its)* is the only personal pronoun that does not refer to persons.

27. A **compound personal pronoun** is formed by adding the suffix *self* or *selves* to the simple pronoun.

> | SINGULAR | PLURAL |
> |---|---|
> | her—herself | them—themselves |
> | him—himself | your—yourselves |
> | my—myself | our—ourselves |

> (But NEVER "hisself" or "theirselves.")

**a.** A compound personal pronoun may be **intensive:** used to show emphasis.

He *himself* is guilty.

**b.** A compound personal pronoun may be **reflexive:** used to refer to the subject.

She voted for *herself*.   (she = herself)

Eric dressed *himself*.   (Eric = himself)

**c.** Unless the pronoun has a clear antecedent, as in the preceding examples, the compound form should not be substituted for the simple form.

> Wrong: The only exercise my sister and *myself* get is running up bills.
> Right:  The only exercise my sister and *I* get is running up bills.

**28.** A **demonstrative pronoun** points out a person, place, or thing.

**a.** The most common demonstrative pronouns are *this*, *that*, *these*, and *those*.

| SINGULAR | PLURAL |
|---|---|
| *This* is my VCR. | *These* are my VCR tapes. |
| *That* is my VCR. | *Those* are my VCR tapes. |

**b.** *This* and *these* = nearby. *That* and *those* = farther away.

**29.** An **indefinite pronoun** refers *indefinitely* to a person, place, or thing.

**a.** Some indefinite pronouns are always SINGULAR.

| another | each | everything | nothing |
|---|---|---|---|
| anybody | either | neither | one |
| anyone | everybody | nobody | somebody |
| anything | everyone | no one | someone |

> Right: *Neither is* my sister.
> Right: *Everyone* in my class *has* a new book.

**b.** Some indefinite pronouns are always PLURAL: *both*, *few*, *many*, *several*.

> Right: "*Many are* called, but *few are* chosen."
> Right: *Several* of the girls *have* been selected for camp.

**c.** Some indefinite pronouns are sometimes singular, sometimes plural.

> ANY:  *Is* any *of the applesauce* left? (singular)
> *Are* any *of the apples* ripe? (plural)

>> Notice: The phrase that follows the indefinite pronoun affects its number.
>> "Applesauce" is a mass: it can't be counted. (Other examples: spinach, grass, cereal.)
>> "Apples" are individuals: they can be counted. (Other examples: dollars, books, potatoes.)

> MOST:  Most of the applesauce *has* been eaten. (singular)
> Most of the apples *have* been eaten. (plural)

> NONE:  None of the applesauce *is* left. (singular)
> None of the apples *are* left. (plural)

> SOME:  Some of the applesauce *has* been eaten. (singular)
> Some of the apples *have* been eaten. (plural)

**30.** A **relative pronoun** introduces a dependent clause and joins the clause to a related word (its antecedent). Common relative pronouns are *who*, *that*, *which*, and *what*. (Dependent clauses are underlined.)

**a.** The following dependent clauses modify a noun and are called *adjective clauses*.

We prayed for the child who fell into the well.

Helen ordered chocolate, which is not on her diet.

I found the sweater (that) you lost.
> (Sometimes the relative pronoun may be omitted, as in this sentence.)

**b.** The relative pronouns *that*, *which*, and *what* have the same form in the nominative and objective cases. *Who*, however, changes form.

> People *who* eat sweets take up two seats!
> > (*Who*, nominative case, is subject of *eat*.)
>
> He is the candidate for *whom* I voted.
> > (*Whom*, objective case, is object of the preposition *for*.)
>
> The woman *whose* trouble is all behind her is probably a school bus driver!
> > (*Whose* is the possessive case.)

**c.** The suffix *ever* when added to *who*, *whom*, *which*, and *what* forms the **compound relative pronouns** *whoever*, *whomever*, *whichever*, and *whatever*.

**d.** A relative pronoun functions as subject or object in its own clause.

> (1) The student who ran the campaign is Fred Smith.
>
> > (*Who* is subject of the verb *ran*.)
>
> (2) The student whom I selected is Fred Smith.
>
> > (*Whom* is object of the verb *selected*.)

**e.** The relative pronoun *who* is always used to refer to persons; *which* to animals or things; and *that* to either persons, places, or things. (See also item 203.)

**f.** *Which* should NEVER be used to refer to a complete clause.

> Wrong: She was absent, *which* caused her to fail the test.
>
> Right: It was her absence *which* caused her to fail the test.
>
> or: She was absent and therefore failed the test.
>
> or: Her absence caused her to fail the test.
>
> or: She failed the test because she was absent.

**31.** An **interrogative pronoun** is used to ask a question. The interrogative pronouns are *who (whom, whose)*, *which*, and *what*.

> *Whose* is this?
> *Which* do you prefer?
> *What* shall we do?

The case of *who*, *whom* depends on the way it is used in a sentence.

> *Who* is going to the party? (subject of the verb *is going*)
> *Who* do you suppose is going to the party? (The interrupter *do you suppose* does not affect the subject–verb agreement of *Who is going*.)
> *Whom* shall we invite? (object of the verb *shall invite*)
> To *whom* did you give the book? (object of the preposition *to*)

**Easy Aid:** If you are uncertain as to whether to use *who* or *whom* in a sentence, change the question to a statement.

> Question: (*Who, Whom*) is going to the party?
> Answer: *She* is going to the party. (*She* is nominative case, so *who* is correct.)

> Question: (*Who, Whom*) shall we invite?
> Answer: We shall invite *her*. (*Her* is objective case, so *whom* is correct.)

> Question: To (*who, whom*) did you give the book?
> Answer: You gave the book to *him*. (*Him* is objective case, so *whom* is correct.)

## 32–35. CASE

**32.** The term **case** is used to explain the relation of a noun or pronoun to the other words in a sentence. There are three cases: *nominative*, *objective*, *possessive*.

**a.** The form of a noun does not change to indicate case, except for the possessive. But the form of a personal pronoun does change according to its use in a sentence.

*Laugh Your Way Through Grammar*

| | NOUN | PRONOUN |
|---|---|---|
| *nominative:* | The *boy* was lost. | *He* was lost. |
| *objective:* | Bill found the *boy*. | Bill found *him*. |
| *possessive:* | The *boy's* parents were alarmed. | *His* parents were alarmed. |

**b.** Study the nominative and objective forms of the personal pronouns.

| | NOMINATIVE | | OBJECTIVE | |
|---|---|---|---|---|
| | SINGULAR | PLURAL | SINGULAR | PLURAL |
| *1st person:* | I | we | me | us |
| *2nd person:* | you | you | you | you |
| *3rd person:* | he | | him | |
| | she | they | her | them |
| | it | | it | |

**33. a.** The **nominative case** is used when the pronoun is the *subject* of a verb.

> (1) *She* received an "A" in her favorite subject—BUY-ology!
> (*She* is subject of the sentence.)

> (2) *I* studied French, and *she* took Spanish.
> (*I* and *she* are subjects of the independent clauses.)

> (3) Rob will visit the Grand Canyon next summer if *he* saves enough money.
> (*He* is subject of the dependent clause "if . . . money.")

**b.** Observe the same rule even when the subject is *compound*. (See also *e* of this section.)

> *Liz* and *I* are going to the skating rink.
> *He* and *Maria* never tell a secret to the rich because money talks!

**Easy Aid:** If you have trouble with the preceding rule, try the elimination trick. For example: (He? Him?) and Maria never tell a secret. Eliminate "and Maria." You would say "He never tells a secret," wouldn't you?

**c.** In an interrogative sentence, change the question to a statement.

> Did (*she, her*) and Frank get married?
> (*She, her*) and Frank did get married.
> > (Now it is clear that *she*, the subject, is correct.)

**d.** A predicate pronoun (7-f) takes the nominative case. A predicate pronoun follows any form of the verb *be*: am, is, are, was, were, been.

> It was *I* who said that finding a doctor today is a matter of course—the golf course! (*It = I.*)
> The expert who told us that a steel ball will bounce higher than a rubber ball was *he*. (*Expert = he*)

The verb *be* functions not only as an *auxiliary verb* (4-e) but also as a *linking verb* (44) because it connects the subject with the predicate pronoun.

**e.** Avoid these common errors in case:

Use the *nominative* case when the subject is compound.

> (1) Wrong: *You* and *me* know that smiles are just like colds—they're catching!
> > (You wouldn't say: *Me* know that . . .)
>
> Right: *You* and *I* know that smiles are just like colds—they're catching!
>
> (2) Wrong: We found courage when *him* and *me* heard that triumph is just "umph" added to "try."
> > (You wouldn't say: *Him* heard that . . . or *Me* heard that . . .)
>
> Right: We found courage when *he* and *I* heard that triumph is just "umph" added to "try."

*Laugh Your Way Through Grammar*

Use the *nominative* case when the predicate pronoun is compound.

(3) Wrong:  The guilty parties are *him* and *me*.
    Right:  The guilty parties are *he* and *I*.

(4) Wrong:  Was it *you* or *her* who said that an accountant is merely a figurehead?
    Right:  Was it *you* or *she* who said that an accountant is merely a figurehead?

**34. a.** The **objective case** is used when the pronoun is the *direct object* of a verb (7-b).

>  The class bully hit *him*.
>  The announcer introduced *them*.
>  The monkey slapped *Jim* and *me*.
>
>>  (compound direct object. You wouldn't say: The monkey slapped *I*.)

**b.** The objective case is used when the pronoun is the *indirect object* (7-c).

>  His mother gave *him* a dollar.
>  The messenger brought *her* a telegram.
>  The monkey gave *Jim* and *me* its banana.
>
>>  (compound indirect object. You wouldn't say: The monkey gave *I* its banana.)

**c.** The objective case is used when the pronoun is the *object of a preposition* (64).

>  According to *him*, a person who knows everything has a lot to learn.
>  Barbara saved some spaghetti for *them*.
>  The monkey shared its banana with *Jim* and *me*.
>
>>  (compound object of a preposition. You wouldn't say: The monkey shared its banana with *I*.)

**d.** Avoid these common errors in case:

Use the *objective* case when the object is compound.

> (1) Wrong: Our teacher congratulated *Tess* and *I* when we defined "comet" as a long-haired star.
>
> Right: Our teacher congratulated *Tess* and *me* when we defined "comet" as a long-haired star.
> (compound direct object)

> (2) Wrong: Their employer gave *she* and *Ben* a day off before the Thanksgiving holiday.
>
> Right: Their employer gave *her* and *Ben* a day off before the Thanksgiving holiday.
> (compound indirect object)

> (3) Wrong: Mother agreed with *Vic* and *I* when we said that a donkey is beautiful to a donkey and a pig to a pig.
>
> Right: Mother agreed with *Vic* and *me* when we said that a donkey is beautiful to a donkey and a pig to a pig.
> (compound object of a preposition)

**35. a.** The **possessive case** is used to show *ownership* or *possession*. The possessive form of a noun (24) contains either an apostrophe alone or an apostrophe and **s** (Jack**'s** coat, Bess' shoes).

**b.** The possessive case of a personal pronoun, on the other hand, NEVER includes an apostrophe (*hers*, not her's; *yours*, not your's; *ours*, not our's; *theirs*, not their's). The possessive case of some indefinite pronouns, however, does require an apostrophe (*one's, anyone's, someone's*).

**c.** When *it's* contains an apostrophe, it is a contraction meaning "it is." The possessive of *it* is *its*.

> Imitation is the sincerest form of flattery—except when *it's* forgery. (contraction)

> The owl can swivel *its* head and look directly backwards. (possessive)

**d.** These are the possessive case forms.

|  | SINGULAR | PLURAL |
|---|---|---|
| *1st person:* | my, mine | our, ours |
| *2nd person:* | your, yours | your, yours |
| *3rd person:* | his | |
| | her, hers | their, theirs |
| | its | |

Some of these pronouns—*my, your, his, her, its, our, their*—are modifiers of nouns, as in 36-a below. Although they are pronouns, they act as adjectives, called *possessive adjectives.*

## 36. AGREEMENT OF PRONOUN AND ANTECEDENT

**a.** The **antecedent** of a pronoun is the word to which the pronoun refers. The pronoun must agree with its antecedent in *gender* and *number.*

> Right: Lucy asked for *her* allowance.
>
> (*Lucy*, the antecedent of *her*, is singular and feminine. So the singular, feminine pronoun *her* is correct.)
>
> Right. They take good care of *their* dogs.
>
> (*They*, the antecedent of *their*, is plural and of common gender—that is, including masculine and feminine. So the plural, common gender pronoun *their* is correct.)

**b.** Use a singular pronoun to refer to a singular *indefinite pronoun* (29-a).

> Right: *Neither* of the boys is going to drive *his* car.
>
> (*Neither* is singular, so the singular pronoun *his* is correct.)

If the indefinite pronoun is plural (29-b), use a plural pronoun.

> Right: *Many* are going to drive *their* cars.
>
> (*Many* is plural, so the plural pronoun *their* is correct.)

**c.** Indefinite pronouns such as *everyone*, *somebody*, and *everybody* may include males and females.

> Problem: Everyone in the class will bring (his? her?) own lunch.
>
> Solution: *Everyone* in the class will bring *his or her* own lunch.

**d.** A pronoun is singular when its antecedent is a noun modified by *each*, *every*, *neither*, or *either*. Although these words are indefinite pronouns (29-a), they are called *indefinite adjectives* when modifying a noun. Don't mistake the indefinite adjective for the real subject.

> *Each* rabbit won *its* owner a blue ribbon.
> s
>
> *Every* boy in the audience had purchased *his* own ticket.
> s
>
> *Either* girl will accept *her* award with grace and modesty.
> s

**e.** If the antecedent of a pronoun is a *collective noun* (22-d), the pronoun is singular if the group acts as a unit, plural if the members of the group act as individuals.

> Right: The jury brought in *its* verdict.
>
> (The members of the jury acted in unison, as one.)
>
> Right: For three hours, the jury exchanged *their* opinions.
>
> (The members of the jury acted individually.)

**f.** A pronoun referring to two antecedents connected by *and* is plural if the antecedents are different persons, animals, or things.

> (1) Jack and Jill lost *their* way.

However, if the two antecedents refer to the same person, the pronoun is singular.

> (2) The captain and quarterback broke *his* ankle.
>
> (The two nouns, *captain* and *quarterback*, name the same person.)

**g.** A pronoun referring to two antecedents connected by *or*, *nor*, *either . . . or*, or *neither . . . nor* may be singular or plural depending on the number of the antecedents. (Note: *neither* may be followed by *nor*, but NEVER by *or*.)

> (1) Either Elsie or Jane will bring *her* Monopoly set.
> (Both *Elsie* and *Jane* are singular. Therefore, the singular pronoun *her* is correct.)

> (2) Neither the girls nor the boys kept *their* promises.
> (Both *boys* and *girls* are plural. Therefore, the plural pronoun *their* is correct.)

When one antecedent is singular and one is plural, the pronoun must agree with the nearer one.

> (3) Neither the *coach* nor his *players* have given *their* consent to the trip.
> (Since *coach* and *players* differ in number, the pronoun *their* correctly refers to the nearer antecedent, *players*.)

> (4) Neither the *players* nor the *coach* has given *his* consent.
> (Since *players* and *coach* differ in number, the pronoun *his* correctly refers to the nearer antecedent, *coach*.)

**h.** Sometimes the antecedent of a pronoun is not clear. Then it is necessary to rewrite the sentence or insert a noun, thus making the antecedent clear.

> (1) Unclear: The teacher told the new student that she needed three books. (Who is *she*: the teacher or the new student?)
> Clear: The teacher said that the new student needed three books.
> or: The teacher said to the new student, "You need three books."
> or: Mrs. Brown told Tim that he needed three books.

(2) Unclear: The boss distributed paychecks to his employees, but some were incorrect. (Are the paychecks or the employees incorrect?)

Clear: The boss distributed paychecks to his employees, but some of the checks were incorrect.

Unclear: He eats too fast, and this gives him a stomachache. (Here the antecedent of *this* is missing.)

Clear: Eating too fast gives him a stomachache.


## 37. COMMON PRONOUN ERRORS

**a.** A pronoun following *than* or *as* may be in the nominative or objective case, depending on the sense of the sentence.

You love my brother better than (I or me).
(There are two ways to interpret its meaning.)
You love my brother better than *I* (love him).
(*I* is correct because it is the subject of the dependent
clause "than I love him.")
or: You love my brother better than (you love) *me*.
(*Me* is correct because it is the object of the dependent
clause "than you love me.")

In the sentences above, either pronoun, *I* or *me*, is possible, depending on your interpretation. Sometimes there is only one possible interpretation.

My sister is taller than (I or me).
My sister is taller *than I (am tall)*.

My sister is as tall as (I or me).
My sister is as tall *as I (am tall)*.


**b.** Never repeat a subject by placing a personal pronoun immediately
after it.

Wrong: My sister *she* is very smart.
Right: My sister is very smart.

*Laugh Your Way Through Grammar*

**c.** A pronoun takes the same case as the noun with which it is in apposition (17).

> Wrong: *Us* girls like ice cream.
> Right: *We* girls like ice cream.
> > (*Girls* identifies *we*. Either *we* or *girls* can stand alone as the subject of the sentence. Therefore, the nominative case form *we* is required.)

> Wrong: Ice cream is enjoyed by *we* girls.
> Right: Ice cream is enjoyed by *us* girls.
> > (*Us* is in apposition with *girls*. Either *us* or *girls* can stand alone as the object of the preposition *by*. Therefore, the objective case form *us* is required.)

**Easy Aid:** If you need help, try the elimination trick. "(We or Us) teenagers are happy." Eliminate *teenagers*—"We are happy" or "Us are happy"? The answer is *We*. Another example: "The PTA praised (we or us) seniors." Eliminate *seniors*—"The PTA praised we" or "The PTA praised us"? The answer is *us*.

**d.** *Them* (objective case) should never be used as the subject of a sentence or as an adjective.

> Wrong: *Them* are my friends.
> Right: *They* are my friends.

> Wrong: I gave *them* books to Sally.
> Right: I gave *those* books to Sally.

**e.** Do not shift from one kind of pronoun to another within the same sentence.

> Wrong: If *someone* really wants to bowl well, *you* should practice at least twice a week.
> Right: If *you* really want to bowl well, *you* should practice at least twice a week.
> or: If *someone* really wants to bowl well, *he or she* should practice at least twice a week.

**f.** *Who* may be used as both a relative pronoun (30) and as an interrogative pronoun (31). *Who* (the nominative form) changes to *whom* in the objective case, and to *whose* in the possessive case. Observe these correct uses.

(1) He is one of those drivers *who* is so polite he honks his horn before he forces you off the road!

> (subject of the dependent clause "who is so polite")

(2) Do you know *who* she is?

> (predicate pronoun after the linking verb *is*)

(3) To *whom* did you say that a wedding ring is a tourniquet worn on the left hand to stop circulation?

> (object of the preposition *to*)

(4) The taxi driver *whom* I flagged down said that the easiest way to kill an hour is to drive around the block!

> (direct object of the dependent clause "whom I flagged down")

(5) *Whose* book is this?

> (The possessive form *whose* must not be confused with *who's*, which is a contraction meaning "who is.")

# VERBS

## 38. THE KEYWORD OF A SENTENCE: THE VERB

A **verb** is a word that expresses *action* (play, work, think) or *state of being* (is, are, become, seem). An action may be mental or physical.

(1) A little experience often *upsets* a lot of theory.

> (*Upsets* is an action verb.)

(2) The farmer *was* cross because someone *stepped* on his corn!

> (*Was* shows state of being; *stepped*—in the dependent clause—shows action.)

(3) The mosquito *bites* the hand that *feeds* it.

> (*Bites* is an action verb in the main clause; *feeds* is an action verb in the dependent clause.)

(4) A smile *is* the whisper of a laugh.

> (*Is* shows state of being.)

(5) He *thought* he had wings and could *fly*; he *was* just "plane" crazy!

> (*Thought* and *fly* are action verbs in the first main clause; *was* shows state of being in the second main clause.)

(6) Why did she *say* that fears *multiply* faster than rabbits?

> (*Say* is an action verb in the main clause; *multiply* is an action verb in the dependent clause.)

## 39, 40. TENSE

**39.** The **tense** of a verb shows the time of an action or state of being.

### SIMPLE TENSES

**a.** The **present tense** expresses action taking place in the present.

| SINGULAR | PLURAL |
|---|---|
| *Person* | |
| 1st: I work | we work |
| 2nd: you work | you work |
| 3rd: he, she, it works | they work |

I work in a factory.
He works on a farm.

**b.** The **past tense** expresses action that took place in the past.

| I worked | we worked |
|---|---|
| you worked | you worked |
| he, she, it worked | they worked |

In the past, I worked in a factory.
Yesterday he worked on a farm.

**c.** The **future tense** expresses action that will take place in the future.

| I shall work | we shall work |
|---|---|
| you will work | you will work |
| he, she, it will work | they will work |

I shall work in a factory next week.
Next week he will work on a farm.

## PERFECT TENSES

**d.** The **present perfect tense** expresses action in the past and continuing to the present.

| | |
|---|---|
| I have worked | we have worked |
| you have worked | you have worked |
| he, she, it has worked | they have worked |

I have worked in a factory for five years.
He has worked on a farm for five years.

**e.** The **past perfect tense** expresses action completed before a certain time in the past.

| | |
|---|---|
| I had worked | we had worked |
| you had worked | you had worked |
| he, she, it had worked | they had worked |

I had worked in a factory before I quit.
He had worked on a farm before his back was injured.

**f.** The **future perfect tense** expresses action that will be completed before a certain time in the future.

| | |
|---|---|
| I shall have worked | we shall have worked |
| you will have worked | you will have worked |
| he, she, it will have worked | they will have worked |

By 1998, I shall have worked in the factory for ten years.
By 1998, he will have worked on the farm for ten years.

**40. a.** Avoid unnecessary shifts in tense.

> Wrong: The children *washed* the dishes in soapy water, and they *rinse* them carefully.
>> (shift from past tense *washed* in the first clause to the present tense *rinse* in the second clause)

Right:　The children *washed* the dishes in soapy water, and they *rinsed* them carefully.

Wrong:　The class *congratulates* Dr. Brown when she *announced* her promotion.
　　　　　　　　　(shift from the present tense *congratulates* in the main clause to the past tense *announced* in the subordinate clause)
Right:　The class *congratulated* Dr. Brown when she *announced* her promotion.

**b.** However, it is necessary to shift from past to present when you are stating an eternal truth.

Wrong:　Columbus discovered that the world *was* round.
　　　　　　　　　(It still is round, isn't it?)
Right:　Columbus discovered that the world *is* round.

## 41. PRINCIPAL PARTS OF VERBS

A verb has three main, or principal, parts—the *present tense*, the *past tense*, and the *past participle*. They are called the **principal parts** of a verb.

**a.** The past tense and the past participle of a **regular verb** are formed by adding "-d" or "-ed" to the present tense.

| PRESENT TENSE | PAST TENSE | PAST PARTICIPLE |
|---|---|---|
| tie | tied | tied |
| die | died | died |
| talk | talked | talked |

Note: The past participle, when preceded by the helping verb *have*, *has*, or *had*, is used to form the perfect tenses (39-d, e, f).

**b.** However, **irregular verbs** do not follow rule *a*, above. Their principal parts must be learned by memorizing them.

| PRESENT | PAST | PAST PARTICIPLE |
|---|---|---|
| am, be | was | been |
| bear (carry) | bore | borne |
| beat | beat | beat, beaten |
| become | became | become |
| begin | began | begun |
| bite | bit | bitten |
| bleed | bled | bled |
| blow | blew | blown |
| break | broke | broken |
| bring | brought | brought |
| build | built | built |
| buy | bought | bought |
| catch | caught | caught |
| choose | chose | chosen |
| come | came | come |
| creep | crept | crept |
| cry | cried | cried |
| deal | dealt | dealt |
| dig | dug | dug |
| dive | dived, dove | dived |
| do | did | done |
| draw | drew | drawn |
| drink | drank | drunk |
| drive | drove | driven |
| dry | dried | dried |
| eat | ate | eaten |
| fall | fell | fallen |
| feed | fed | fed |
| feel | felt | felt |
| fight | fought | fought |
| find | found | found |
| flee | fled | fled |
| fly | flew | flown |
| forget | forgot | forgotten |
| forgive | forgave | forgiven |
| freeze | froze | frozen |
| fry | fried | fried |
| get | got | got, gotten |
| give | gave | given |
| go | went | gone |

| PRESENT | PAST | PAST PARTICIPLE |
|---------|------|-----------------|
| grow | grew | grown |
| hang (person) | hanged | hanged |
| hang (picture) | hung | hung |
| has, have | had | had |
| hear | heard | heard |
| hide | hid | hidden |
| know | knew | known |
| lay | laid | laid |
| lead | led | led |
| lie (recline) | lay | lain |
| lie (tell an un-truth) | lied | lied |
| lose | lost | lost |
| make | made | made |
| mean | meant | meant |
| meet | met | met |
| pay | paid | paid |
| ride | rode | ridden |
| ring | rang | rung |
| rise | rose | risen |
| run | ran | run |
| see | saw | seen |
| shake | shook | shaken |
| shine (polish) | shined | shined |
| shine (light) | shone | shone |
| show | showed | shown |
| shrink | shrank | shrunk |
| sing | sang | sung |
| sink | sank | sunk |
| sit | sat | sat |
| slay | slew | slain |
| sleep | slept | slept |
| speak | spoke | spoken |
| spend | spent | spent |
| spring | sprang | sprung |
| stand | stood | stood |
| steal | stole | stolen |
| sting | stung | stung |
| swear | swore | sworn |
| swim | swam | swum |

*Laugh Your Way Through Grammar*

| PRESENT | PAST | PAST PARTICIPLE |
|---------|------|-----------------|
| swing | swung | swung |
| take | took | taken |
| teach | taught | taught |
| tear | tore | torn |
| tell | told | told |
| think | thought | thought |
| throw | threw | thrown |
| try | tried | tried |
| wake | woke (waked) | waked |
| wear | wore | worn |
| win | won | won |
| write | wrote | written |

**c.** A few irregular verbs do not change at all, regardless of tense: burst, burst, burst; hurt, hurt, hurt; spread, spread, spread.

**d.** Misusing the principal parts of verbs results in serious blunders, such as: "We seen it," "He done it," "I have ate." Below are the forms and usage of three irregular verbs. Use these as a guide for other irregular verbs.

**Principal parts: see, saw, seen**

Present tense:    We *see* it.
Past tense:       We *saw* it. (not *seen*)
Past participle:  We *have seen* it.

**Principal parts: do, did, done**

Present tense:    He *does* it.
Past tense:       He *did* it. (not *done*)
Past participle:  He *had done* it. (not *had did*)

**Principal parts: eat, ate, eaten**

Present tense:    I *eat* lobster.
Past tense:       I *ate* lobster.
Past participle:  I *have eaten* lobster. (not *have ate*)

Note: The past participle is always preceded by the helping verb *have*, *has*, or *had*.

## 42, 43. TRANSITIVE AND INTRANSITIVE VERBS

**42. a. Transitive** verbs take a direct object; **intransitive** verbs do not.

**b.** A **transitive verb** requires a *direct object* (7-b) to express a complete thought.

> In 1518 Cortez *brought* seventeen horses to the Western Hemi-
> <sub>d.o.</sub>
> sphere.

> George Washington *named* his favorite horse ''Blue Skin.''
> <sub>d.o.</sub>

**43. a.** An **intransitive verb** does not take a direct object.

> A carrier pigeon with its ears stuffed up cannot *fly*.   (no object)

> Fish *cough*.   (no object)

**b.** Some verbs are transitive in one sentence and intransitive in another.

> Max *wrote* a novel.
> transitive      d.o.

> Max *wrote* rapidly.   (no object)
> intransitive

## 44. LINKING VERBS

**a.** A **linking verb** connects the subject with a word in the predicate: a *noun*, a *pronoun*, or an *adjective*. A linking verb never takes a direct object.

> I *am* a student. (*I* and *student* refer to the same person.)
> (*Student* is a **predicate noun.**)

> I *am* intelligent. (*I* and *intelligent* refer to the same person.)
> (*Intelligent* is a **predicate adjective.**)

**b.** A pronoun that follows a linking verb is in the *nominative case* (33-d).

> The best pitcher on the team *is* she. (*Pitcher* and *she* refer to the same person. *She* is a **predicate pronoun.**)

**c.** The most common linking verbs are forms of the verb *be*: am, is, are, was, were, been. Others: appear, become, feel, grow, look, prove, remain, seem, smell, sound, taste, turn.

> She *became* a ballerina.
> The contestants *seem* clever.

**d.** Sometimes it is difficult to decide whether a verb performs in a sentence as a linking verb or as an action verb. If the verb can be replaced by some form of *be*, then it is a linking verb.

> The pecan pie *tastes* good.
>> (We can substitute a form of *be* as follows:)
> The pecan pie *is* good.
>> (This sentence makes sense; therefore, *tastes* must be a linking verb.)

> Kim *tastes* the pecan pie.
>> (Can we substitute a form of *be* for *tastes*?)
> Kim *is* the pecan pie.
>> (This sentence doesn't make sense; therefore, *tastes* must be an action verb.)

## 45. VOICE

The **voice** of a verb tells whether (*a*) the subject is the actor, or (*b*) the subject is acted upon. Only a transitive verb (42-a) has voice.

**a.** **Active voice** shows the subject is doing the action.

> The author Tobias Smollett *invented* the street-corner mailbox.
> In 1924 Simon & Schuster *published* the first book of crossword puzzles.

**b. Passive voice** shows the subject is receiving the action.

> The street-corner mailbox *was invented* by the author Tobias Smollett.
>
> The first book of crossword puzzles *was published* by Simon & Schuster in 1924.

(Notice that the passive voice requires a form of the verb *be* plus the past participle. Whenever possible, when you are writing, use the active voice.)

**c.** Do not shift from the active voice to the passive voice within the same sentence.

> Wrong:  As we wander through the forest, many small
> active
>
> animals and birds *are seen*.
> passive
>
> > (The active voice *wander* in the subordinate clause shifts to the passive voice *are seen* in the main clause.)
>
> Right:  As we *wander* through the forest, we *see* many
> active                                         active
>
> small animals and birds.

> Wrong:  As Jake *chewed* on the taffy, a tooth *was broken*.
> active                                passive
>
> Right:  As Jake *chewed* on the taffy, he *broke* a tooth.
> active                           active

## 46. MOOD

The **mood** of a verb indicates the manner of expressing an action or state of being.

**a.** The **indicative mood** makes a statement of fact or asks a question.

> He is going to the store.
> Is she going to the store?

**b.** The **imperative mood** gives a command.

Please go to the store immediately.

**c.** The **subjunctive mood** makes a statement that is doubtful or contrary to fact.

(1) Use *were* instead of *was* for the present tense.

Wrong: If I *was* a fish, I would point out that fishing turns men into liars.
Right: If I *were* a fish, I would point out that fishing turns men into liars.

Wrong: She acted as if she *was* still class president.
Right: She acted as if she *were* still class president.

(2) Use *had* and the past participle for the past tense.

Wrong: If I *would have known* the answer, I would have written it.
Right: If I *had known* the answer, I would have written it.

Wrong: If Noah *would have thought* of it when he entered the ark, he would have said, "After me, the deluge!"
Right: If Noah *had thought* of it when he entered the ark, he would have said, "After me, the deluge!"

**d.** Avoid unnecessary shifts in mood.

Wrong: <u>Clean your room</u> and then <u>you may rest.</u>
  *imperative*        *indicative*

(shift from imperative to indicative)

Right: <u>Clean your room</u>, and then <u>rest.</u>
  *imperative*        *imperative*

Right: <u>After you clean your room,</u> <u>you may rest.</u>
  *indicative*        *indicative*

Wrong: <u>You may have ice cream</u> and <u>be quiet</u>.
     *indicative*        *imperative*

(shift from indicative to imperative)

Right: <u>If you are quiet</u>, <u>you may have ice cream</u>.
     *indicative*       *indicative*

## 47. AGREEMENT OF SUBJECT AND VERB

A verb must agree with its subject in (*a*) person and (*b*) number.

**a.** PERSON. A first person subject requires a verb in the first person. Similarly, a second person subject takes a verb in the second person; and a third person subject requires a verb in the third person. (See also 39-a to f.)

   Wrong: I wants chocolate.
   Right:  I want chocolate. (first person)

   Wrong: You was wrong.
   Right:  You were wrong. (second person)

   Wrong: It don't matter.
   Right:  It doesn't matter. (third person)

**b.** NUMBER. A singular subject takes a singular verb; a plural subject takes a plural verb.

   The Model-T *Ford was* seven feet high.
   Blue *whales are* the biggest animals the world has ever known.

A complement (7) does not affect subject-verb agreement. For example, a singular subject requires a singular verb even if the complement is plural.

     My favorite *fruit is* apples.
        *sing.*    *pl.*

   But: *Apples are* my favorite fruit.
     *pl.*        *sing.*

**c.** A few nouns that are plural in form are singular in meaning. Such nouns as *news*, *politics*, *physics*, and *mathematics* take singular verbs.

> *News is* "history shot on the wing." (Gene Fowler)
> *Politics teaches* people to use ballots instead of bullets.

**Mistakes in agreement occur when the subject is compound. Should the verb be singular or plural?**

**d.** A **compound subject** joined by *and* is plural.

> Nessie *and* Champ *are* well-known monsters.

**e.** If a compound subject joined by *and* names the SAME person or thing, the verb is singular.

> Our math teacher and track coach *has* retired.
>> (one person)

BUT: Repeat *our* before *track* if the two subject words refer to different persons or things.

> Our math teacher and OUR track coach *have* retired.
>> (two persons)

**f.** A compound subject joined by *or*; *either . . . or*; or *neither . . . nor* is singular if the two subject words are singular.

> *Nessie* or *Champ is* my favorite monster.
> Either *Nessie* or *Champ is* my favorite monster.
> Neither *Big Foot* nor *Yeti is* my favorite monster.

BUT: The verb is plural if the subject words are plural.

> *Are* either *cats* or *dogs* considered monsters?
> Neither *cats* nor *dogs are* considered monsters.

**g.** If the compound subject joined by *either . . . or*; or *neither . . . nor*; or by *or* or *nor* is made up of one singular word and one plural word, the number is governed by the NEARER subject word.

> Either Jack or his *brothers are* guilty.
> Either his brothers or *Jack is* guilty.

> Neither Jack nor his *sisters sing*.
> Neither his sisters nor *Jack sings*.

**A prepositional phrase (65) within a sentence puzzles a writer. Which is the real subject? How does the phrase affect agreement?**

**h.** A phrase between the subject and the verb does not ordinarily affect the agreement of subject and verb. The subject precedes the phrase; the object of the preposition at the end of the phrase is NOT the subject, as shown in the following examples.

In the jungle, one (of every four lion cubs) starves to death.
<br>               *s*          *phrase*        *v*

(In this example, the verb *starves* agrees with the singular subject, *one*, NOT with the plural object of the preposition, *cubs*.

The eyelashes (of almost any elephant) are four inches long.
<br>    *s*           *phrase*        *v*

(In this example, the verb *are* agrees with the plural subject, *eyelashes*, NOT with the singular object of the preposition, *elephant*.

**i.** If the subject is *plenty*, *abundance*, *variety*, or *rest*, the verb agrees with the object of the preposition. (This is an exception to *h* above.)

> Plenty of *people are* going.   (*people* is plural)
> Plenty of *spinach is* grown here. (*spinach* is singular)

> The rest of the *boys were* rescued. (*boys* is plural)
> The rest of the *candy was* lost. (*candy* is singular)

**j.** If a prepositional phrase is followed by a *relative pronoun* (30), the verb of the dependent clause must agree with the antecedent of the relative pronoun. Occasionally, it is difficult to determine the antecedent; then you must look closely at the *meaning* of the sentence.

Mary is one (*of the girls*) who are helping.

> (All the girls are helping, and Mary is just one of them. The antecedent of the relative pronoun *who* is *girls*, which is plural. Therefore, *are* is correct.)

BUT: Mary is *the* one (*of the girls*) who is helping.

> (The article *the* changes the meaning of the sentence by indicating that Mary is the only one who is helping. The antecedent of *who* is *one*, which is singular. Therefore, *is* is correct.)

**k.** Ignore expressions as the following when they come between the subject and the verb: *accompanied by, as well as, including, in addition to, no less than, together with, not* . . . . Such phrases do NOT affect the agreement of subject and verb.

*Mary*, (together with her sisters,) *is going.*
s

*Mary and John*, (as well as Mary's sister,) *are going.*
s                                                    v

Her *expression*, (not her words,) *is* friendly.
s                              v

Her *words*, (not her expression,) *are* friendly.
s                              v

**Indefinite pronouns cause trouble. Which ones are singular, and which are plural?**

**l.** If an *indefinite pronoun* (29) is the subject, the verb will be singular or plural depending on the number of the pronoun. Remember: most indefinite pronouns are singular (*each, one, neither, someone, everybody*), but a few are plural (*both, many, several*).

(1) *Singular indefinite pronouns:*

> *Everybody knows* that few children fear water unless soap is added.

> *Nobody* ever *gets* hurt on the corners of a square deal.

> *Is everyone* going?

> *Each* of his patients *is* saying that the new doctor is so mean that he keeps his stethoscope in the freezer!

> *Everybody* on the marriage council *insists* that snoring is "sheet music"!

(2) *Plural indefinite pronouns*:

> "*Many are* called, but *few are* chosen."

> *Several* of the female joggers *have* a whim to be slim!

> *Both* of the youngsters *think* that PTA means "Poor Tired Adults"!

**Mathematical expressions can be tricky.**

**m.** Study these examples:

> Four times two are eight.
> Four and two are six.
> Four plus two is six.
> Four minus two is two.
> Four divided by two is two.
> One-fourth of four is one.

**n.** If a noun indicates a measurement of space, time, or money, it is singular in meaning, even if it looks plural.

> Ten *dollars* is the price he quoted.
> Thirty *minutes* is all the time I can give you.
> Five *miles* is the distance from Tantown to Tooley.

**o.** If the subject is a fraction and is followed by an *of*-phrase, the verb agrees with the object of the preposition. (This is another exception to rule *h* of this section.)

One-fourth (of the *pizza*) *was* consumed.

One-fourth (of the *sandwiches*) *were* consumed.

**p.** The expression "*a* number of" takes a plural verb.

> *A number of* children *are* going to the picnic.
>
> *A number of* the team *are* coming with me.

BUT: "*the* number of" takes a singular verb.

> *The number of* children going to the picnic *is* sixteen.
>
> *The number of* the team who may come with me *is* limited to five.

**Other problems in agreement:**

**q.** A collective noun (22-d) takes a singular verb when the group is acting as a unit, and a plural verb when the individuals are acting independently.

> (1) The *team is* playing today in Hempstead.
>
> ("team" acting as one, together)
>
> (2) BUT: The *team are* voting today for a new captain.
>
> ("team" acting as individuals)
>
> (3) The *class was* taught by Mr. Jones.
>
> (4) BUT: The *class were* discussing the parts of speech.

**r.** *It* always takes a singular verb even when followed by a plural predicate noun or pronoun.

> *It is* not the anchor *people* who gather the news.
> *It is they* who do.

BUT: *you* requires a plural verb even when the person addressed is singular.

> Albert, *you were* late.


**s.** In some sentences beginning with *there is* (*are*) or *here is* (*are*), the introductory word *here* or *there* is an *expletive*, NOT the subject. The subject follows the verb.

> There *is* a monster called the Abominable Snowman in the Himalaya Mountains.
>
> > (In subject-verb order: A monster called the Abominable Snowman is in the Himalaya Mountains.)
>
> There *are* monsters called Skunk Apes living in the Florida swamp.
>
> > (In subject-verb order: Monsters called Skunk Apes are living in the Florida swamp.)


**t.** In other sentences beginning with *there is* (*are*) or *here is* (*are*), the introductory word *here* or *there* is an adverb.

> *There* is my bus.
> adv.
>
> > (In subject-verb order: My bus is there.)
>
> *Here* are my cash and my credit card.
> adv.
>
> > (In subject-verb order: My cash and my credit card are here.)

## 48–51. VERBALS

**Verbals** are words that begin as verbs but change both in form and in use. There are three kinds of verbals: *infinitives*, *participles*, and *gerunds*.

**48. a.** An **infinitive** is a verbal formed by combining *to* and a verb.

| | | |
|---|---|---|
| to play | to be | to smile |
| to joke | to have | to jump |

Try to avoid splitting infinitives.

Wrong:  He is going *to quickly swallow* the medicine.
Right:   He is going *to swallow* the medicine quickly.

Wrong:  She dared *to boldly accuse* me.
Right:   She dared *to accuse* me boldly.

**b.** An infinitive may take a subject, an object, or a modifier.

Mother urged *us* to eat.
    (*Us* is the subject of *to eat.*)

Ms. Lopez asked the class to write a *poem.*
    (*Poem* is the object of *to write.*)

She told us to start *immediately.*
    (*Immediately* modifies *to start.*)

**c.** An infinitive plus one or more words forms an **infinitive phrase.** In a sentence, the phrase acts as a single unit—as a noun, an adjective, or an adverb.

**d.** An infinitive used as a *noun* may be a subject, object, predicate noun, or appositive.

SUBJECT:

"*To err* is human."   (infinitive)
*To milk a cow* is my leading ambition.   (phrase)

DIRECT OBJECT:

> They prefer *to smile*.   (infinitive)
> His mother said that she would like *to see some change in him*—so he swallowed two nickels and a dime.   (phrase)

OBJECT OF PREPOSITION:

> He asked for nothing except *to read*.   (infinitive)
> He asked for nothing except *to read the Bible and the Times*.   (phrase)

PREDICATE NOUN:

> Life is *to live*. (infinitive)
> Happiness is *to love and to be loved by the same person*.   (phrase)

APPOSITIVE:

> She described her goal, *to climb*.
> (infinitive in apposition with *goal*, the direct object)
> His wish, *to become a flight attendant*, may well come true.
> (phrase in apposition with *wish*, the subject)

**e.** An infinitive used as an *adjective* modifies a noun or pronoun; when used as an *adverb*, the infinitive modifies a verb or an adjective.

ADJECTIVE:

> Give me a riddle *to solve*.
> (infinitive modifying *riddle*, the direct object.)
> The horse *to be auctioned* had won the Derby.
> (phrase modifying *horse*, the subject)

ADVERB:

> Are you ready *to leave*?
> (infinitive modifying *ready*, an adjective)
> Sally dived *to save the drowning child*.
> (phrase modifying *dived*, a verb)

*Laugh Your Way Through Grammar*

**f.** The subject of an infinitive is in the objective case.

> The coach ordered *them* to do twenty push-ups.
> The monkey begged *Jim* and *me* to return its banana.

**g.** The object of an infinitive is in the objective case.

> I was asked to call *her*.
> Judd wanted to tell *me* that an acrobat turns a flop into a success.

**h.** The *to* of the infinitive is frequently omitted after certain verbs: dare, feel, hear, let, make, need, and see.

> A roller coaster can make your blood *(to) race* and your legs *(to) tremble*.
> I saw him *(to) go*.

**49.** A **participle** is a verbal used as an *adjective*.

**a.** The **present participle** is formed by adding -*ing* to the stem of the verb: *eating, talking, walking*. The **past participle** is formed by adding *d* or -*ed* to the stem. The past participle is the third principal part of a verb (41): smile, smiled, *have smiled*; learn, learned, *have learned*. Some verbs are irregular: go, went, *have gone*.

**b.** A participle, when used alone, is a **pure adjective:** *fallen* leaves, *yelping* dog, *stored* energy.

> The *whistling* boy entered the auditorium.
> (The participle *whistling* modifies *boy*.)

**c.** A participle in the predicate, following a linking verb (44-a), is called a **predicate adjective.**

> The child was *frightened*.
> (The participle *frightened* modifies *child*.)

**d.** When used with other words, the participle forms a **participial phrase,** modifying a noun or pronoun.

> This novel, *written by Willa Cather*, was immediately popular.
>> (The participial phrase "written by Willa Cather" modifies *novel*.)

**e. Punctuation Aid:**

(1) A participial phrase appearing at the BEGINNING of a sentence is separated by a comma from the rest of the sentence.

> *Parked alongside a hydrant,* the car was ticketed.
> *Singing loudly,* we entered the auditorium.

(2) A participial phrase that appears in the MIDDLE of a sentence is set off by commas *if the phrase is not necessary to the meaning of the sentence.* (See 224-1.)

> The little boy, *fiddling with some marbles,* boldly challenged the class bully.
>> ("Fiddling with some marbles" is not necessary to the meaning of the sentence and therefore is set off with commas.)

(3) If the phrase is *necessary* to the meaning of the sentence, it is NOT set off with commas.

> The little boy *fiddling with marbles* is my brother.
>> ("Fiddling with marbles" identifies the little boy who is my brother and therefore is necessary and is not set off with commas.)

**50. a.** A **gerund** is a verbal used as a *noun*. It is formed by adding *-ing* to the stem of the verb: *dancing, chewing, walking*, etc. Don't confuse a gerund with a present participle, which also ends in *-ing*. Remember: a participle functions as an *adjective*, a gerund as a *noun*.

**b.** A gerund plus one or more words forms a **gerund phrase** used as a noun.

SUBJECT:

> *Blushing* is a lost art.   (gerund)
> *Swallowing your pride* is good for you—and it contains no
>    calories!   (phrase)

DIRECT OBJECT:

> Many children love *swimming*.   (gerund)
> I heard the *whispering of the wind in the trees*.   (phrase)

OBJECT OF PREPOSITION:

> She dreamed of *dancing*.   (gerund)
> They went to the Met for the *opening of the new opera sea-
>    son*.   (phrase)

PREDICATE NOUN:

> Her favorite hobby is *ice-skating*.   (gerund)
> His favorite hobby is *making model airplanes*.   (phrase)

APPOSITIVE:

> Her work, *teaching*, meant more to her than anything
>    else.   (gerund)
> She loved her work, *teaching ceramics to small chil-
>    dren*.   (phrase)

**c.** A noun or pronoun preceding a gerund usually takes the possessive
case. (35)

> We admired *Fran's handling* of the case.
> He liked *my singing*.
> His mother did not approve of *his going* away.

Be sure to draw a distinction between a gerund and a present participle, since both verbals end in *-ing*. Imagine three boys acting. Someone asks: "Which boy do you like best?" You answer:

> "I like the boy acting in Scene I."

The speaker likes the *boy*; *acting* is a participle identifying him.

Someone asks: "What do you like best about that boy?" You answer:

"I like the boy's acting in Scene I."

This time the speaker likes the *acting* rather than the boy; *acting* is a gerund.

### d. Punctuation Aid:

A **gerund phrase** that is the subject and that appears at the beginning of a sentence is not separated by a comma from the rest of the sentence.

*Studying for two hours* helped me to pass the test.
(subject; no comma)

## 51. DANGLING VERBAL PHRASES

A **dangling modifier** occurs when a phrase has no *logical* subject to modify. The fault can be corrected by supplying a logical "doer" of the action.

(1) Wrong: Standing on a corner, two cars were seen to collide. (Obviously ridiculous: imagine two cars standing on a corner!)

Right: Standing on a corner, **we** saw two cars collide. (Now the phrase, "Standing on a corner," modifies the pronoun *we*, and the sentence makes sense.)

(2) Wrong: By studying for two hours, the test was passed. (Who studied? Who passed the test? Did the "test" do the studying?)

Right: By studying for two hours, **I** passed the test. (Now the pronoun *I* indicates who did the "studying for two hours," and the sentence makes sense.)

(3) Wrong: To play football well, running, kicking, and passing exams are necessary. (Who is playing football?)

Right: To play football well, **one** must run, kick, and pass exams! (Now the pronoun *one* indicates who might want "to play football well," and the sentence makes sense.)

# ADJECTIVES

## 52. A MODIFIER: THE ADJECTIVE

An **adjective** is a modifier (8). As a modifier, an adjective describes or limits the meaning of a noun or pronoun.

> **descriptive adjectives:**
>
> > a *beautiful* sunset,
> > *spectacular* fireworks,
> > an *inspiring* message
>
> **limiting adjectives:**
>
> > *ten* days, *this* antique, a *few* seniors

## 53. WORDS THAT FUNCTION AS ADJECTIVES

Nouns, pronouns, articles, numerals, and participles—all can function as adjectives.

**a.** *common nouns:* a *city* street, a *family* gathering, a *diamond* ring

**b.** *proper nouns:* the *Canadian* capital, the *Mexican* border, the *American* flag (Note: Adjectives formed from proper nouns are called **proper adjectives.** They are always capitalized.)

**c.** *possessive forms of nouns and pronouns: Carla's* school, *her* graduation

**d.** *demonstrative pronouns: this* book, *that* song, *these* apples, *those* trees

**e.** *indefinite pronouns: each* girl, *every* boy, *another* reason

**f.** *interrogative pronouns: whose* jacket, *which* team, *what* time

**g.** *indefinite articles: a, an*; *definite article: the*

**h.** *numerals: five* children, the *fifth* child

**i.** *participles: falling* star, *cracked* egg, *broken* glass

## 54. POSITION OF ADJECTIVES

**a.** As a rule, an adjective precedes the noun it modifies.

a *good* day; the *next* chapter; a *tall*, *attractive* girl

**b.** A combination of adjectives may follow the noun.

All citizens, *rich* or *poor*, are expected to vote.
The hikers, *tired* but *happy*, returned at midnight.
The principal, *strong*, *clever*, and *charming*, won the budget debate.

(Notice that commas are placed before and after the series of adjectives in the above sentences.)

**c.** An adjective, called the **predicate adjective** (44-a), may be placed in the predicate of a sentence to modify the subject noun or pronoun.

Margaret was *absent* today.

I am very *thirsty*.

## 55. DEGREES OF COMPARISON OF ADJECTIVES

Adjectives have three **degrees of comparison:** *positive*, *comparative*, and *superlative*.

**a.** The **positive degree** simply expresses a quality.

Jake is *tall*.
Jill is *intelligent*.

**b.** The **comparative degree** expresses a lower or higher degree than the positive. It draws a comparison between *two* people or objects. It is formed by adding "-er" or "more" to the positive form.

Jake is the *taller* of the two boys.
Jill is the *more (less) intelligent* of the two girls.

**c.** The **superlative degree** expresses the lowest or highest degree. It draws a comparison among *three* or more people or objects. It is formed by adding "-est" or "most" to the positive form.

> Jake is the *tallest* of the nine boys.
> Jill is the *most (least) intelligent* of the eight girls.

**d.** A few adjectives form their comparative and superlative degrees in an irregular way.

| POSITIVE | COMPARATIVE | SUPERLATIVE |
|----------|-------------|-------------|
| bad | worse | worst |
| far | farther, further | farthest, furthest |
| good | better | best |
| ill | worse | worst |
| little | less | least |
| many | more | most |
| much | more | most |
| several | more | most |
| some | more | most |
| well | better | best |

**e.** If an adjective expresses an absolute quality, it should not be compared. For example: the adjective *perfect* expresses an absolute quality. There is no such thing as "more perfect" or "less perfect." Instead, use *more nearly* or *most nearly.*

> Wrong: This is the *most perfect* circle I've drawn.
> Right: This is the *most nearly perfect* circle I've drawn.

Other absolutes: *unique*; *dead*; *endless*; *square*; *straight*; *inevitable*; *current.*

> Wrong: This is a most unique experience.
> Right: This is a *unique* experience.

> Wrong: The class seemed more endless than usual.
> Right: The class seemed *endless*, as usual.

**f.** Use ''as . . . as'' for positive comparisons, and ''so . . . as'' for negative comparisons.

> Positive:  Leona is *as* pretty *as* Nell.
> Negative:  Leona is not *so* pretty *as* Nell.

## 56. COMMON ADJECTIVE ERRORS

**a.** Most one- and two-syllable adjectives ending in *y* form their comparative and superlative degrees in the regular manner: add -er and -est to the positive. First, though, change *y* to *i*, as below.

| POSITIVE | COMPARATIVE | SUPERLATIVE |
|----------|-------------|-------------|
| happy | happier | happiest |
| pretty | prettier | prettiest |
| dry | drier | driest |
| lovely | lovelier | loveliest |
| silly | sillier | silliest |
| noisy | noisier | noisiest |
| easy | easier | easiest |

**b.** When the comparative degree of an adjective is used with *than*, the words *other* or *else* must be used also.

> Wrong:  He is taller than any boy in his class.
> Right:   He is taller than any *other* boy in his class.

Use common sense on this one: He cannot be taller than any boy in his class, since *he* is in his class. But he can be taller than any *other* boy in his class.

> Wrong:  That man is richer than any man in America.
> Right:   That man is richer than any *other* man in America.

(But it is correct to write: ''That woman is richer than any man in America.'')

**c.** Avoid the **double comparison** error. Add either ''-er'' or ''more'' to an adjective to form the comparative degree (55-b), but do not use both methods together. The same rule applies when forming the superlative degree (55-c).

>Wrong:  Jake is the *more taller* of the two boys.
>Right:    Jake is the *taller* of the two boys.

>Wrong:  Jake is the *most tallest* of the nine boys.
>Right:    Jake is the *tallest* of the nine boys.

**d.** When an adjective and a noun are combined to form a compound adjective, use the singular form of the noun.

>The teacher gave her students a forty-*minute* recess.
>They built a six-*foot* wall around their home.

BUT . . .

>The recess was forty *minutes* long.
>The wall is six *feet* high.

**Easy Aid:** If the modifier comes BEFORE the noun, it should be singular. If the modifier comes AFTER the noun, it should be plural.

**e.** Some nouns keep their SINGULAR form when preceded by an adjective expressing a number. (Examples: *dozen, gross, score, head, hundred, million, thousand .*)

>I would like *three dozen* eggs. (not three dozens)
>There are *two million* stars in the sky. (not two millions)
>The manager ordered *six gross* of pencils. (not six grosses)

When the number is not specified, the PLURAL form should be used.

>*Dozens* of eggs flooded the market.
>There are *millions* of stars in the sky.
>*Grosses* of pencils are still in the storehouse.

**f.** When two or more adjectives or nouns refer to the SAME person or thing, use an article (*a*, *an*, *the*) before the first adjective or noun only.

> We purchased the white and green house.
>
> > (one house)
>
> The red, white, and blue flag is ours.
>
> > (one flag)
>
> The doberman and shepherd is mine.
>
> > (one dog, part doberman, part shepherd)
>
> John is a waiter and busboy.
>
> > (one person doing two jobs)

When two or more adjectives or nouns refer to DIFFERENT persons or things, use an article before each adjective or noun.

> We purchased the white and the green house.
>
> > (two houses)
>
> A red, a white, and a blue flag flew over the stadium.
>
> > (three flags)
>
> The doberman and the shepherd are popular dogs.
>
> > (two dogs)
>
> A waiter and a busboy hovered over our table.
>
> > (two persons)

**g.** Use *a* before a noun beginning with a consonant. Use *an* before a noun beginning with a vowel.

> He bought a giraffe, an elephant, and a hound.
> An apple, an orange, and a pear are in the refrigerator.

# ADVERBS

## 57, 58. ANOTHER MODIFIER: THE ADVERB

An **adverb** describes or limits the meaning of a verb, an adjective, or another adverb. Like the adjective, an adverb is a modifier (8).

## 57. An adverb modifies a verb.

An adverb may be placed before a verb, after a verb, or within a verb phrase.

*Usually* the game of love *ends* in a tie.
 adv.                            v

Ideas die *quickly* in some heads because they can't stand sol-
 v       adv.

itary confinement!

Ida has *frequently* performed for our troops.
        adv.
        └──── verb phrase ────┘

## 58. An adverb may modify an adjective or another adverb.

MODIFYING AN ADJECTIVE:

She is *exceedingly* intelligent.
        adv.            adj.

The *rather* futile effort failed.
     adv.    adj.

MODIFYING AN ADVERB:

He writes *very cleverly*.
     *adv.*      *adv.*

Don't row *too far* from shore.
       *adv. adv.*

## 59. ADVERBS EXPRESS TIME, PLACE, DEGREE, MANNER

**a.** Adverbs may be classified according to meaning.

TIME adverbs answer the question WHEN.
     yesterday, today, now, later

PLACE adverbs answer the question WHERE.
     here, there, inside, nowhere

DEGREE adverbs answer the question TO WHAT EXTENT.
     more, less, rather, very

MANNER adverbs answer the question HOW.
     politely, stubbornly, happily, surely

**b.** A noun may be used as an adverb of TIME or PLACE.

We will leave *Monday* for Washington.
          *n.*

   (*Monday*, a noun used as an adverb, modifies the verb
   *will leave*.)

When will you come *home*?
               *n.*

   (*Home*, a noun used as an adverb, modifies the verb
   *will come*.)

## 60. FORMING ADVERBS FROM ADJECTIVES

**a.** Many adverbs are formed by adding *-ly* to adjectives.

| ADJECTIVE | ADVERB |
|---|---|
| usual | usually |
| beautiful | beautifully |
| scarce | scarcely |
| happy | happily |
| angry | angrily |

**b. Spelling Aids:**

(1) The regular rule: add *-ly* directly to the adjective.

scarce—scarcely

(2) When adding *-ly* to an adjective ending in *l*, be sure to keep the *-l* ending of the adjective.

usual—usually

(3) When adding *ly* to an adjective ending in *y*, change the *y* to *i*.

angry—angrily

## 61. INTERROGATIVE ADVERBS

An **interrogative adverb** begins a question.

*Where* are they going?
They are going *where*? (subject-verb order)

(*Where* modifies the verb *are going*.)

*How* are you going to ice the cake?
*Why* did you do it?
*When* will he graduate?

## 62. DEGREES OF COMPARISON OF ADVERBS

Adverbs, like adjectives, have **degrees of comparison:** *positive, comparative,* and *superlative.* The rules for comparing adverbs are the same as those for comparing adjectives (55).

**a.** The **positive degree** simply states a quality.

> Dick drove *carefully.*
> Jane drove *fast.*

**b.** The **comparative degree** expresses a lower or higher degree than the positive. It draws a comparison between *two* people or objects. It is formed by adding ''-er'' or ''more'' to the positive form.

> Dick drove *more (less) carefully* than Jane.
> Jane drove *faster* than Dick.

**c.** The **superlative degree** expresses the lowest or highest degree. It draws a comparison among *three* or more people or objects. It is formed by adding ''-est'' or ''most'' to the positive form.

> Of the three contestants, Dick drove the *most (least) carefully.*
> Of the four contestants, Jane drove the *fastest.*

**d.** A few adverbs form their comparative and superlative degrees in an irregular way.

| POSITIVE | COMPARATIVE | SUPERLATIVE |
|----------|-------------|-------------|
| badly | worse | worst |
| far | farther, further | farthest, furthest |
| little | less | least |
| much | more | most |
| well | better | best |

## 63. COMMON ADVERB ERRORS

**a.** Be sure to use the correct form of the following adverbs:

| WRONG | RIGHT |
|---|---|
| anywheres | anywhere |
| somewheres | somewhere |
| nowheres | nowhere |
| firstly | first |

**b.** Don't use a negative to split an infinitive.

Wrong: I chose *to* not *go* to class.
Right: I chose not *to go* to class.

**c.** *No* and *not* (*n't*) are, of course, negatives. So are "never, hardly, scarcely, neither, nobody, nothing, none." Avoid the **double negative.**

Wrong: I am not in no shape to exercise.
Right: I am not in *any* shape to exercise.
Right: I am in no shape to exercise.

Wrong: Nobody never tells me what's going on.
Right: Nobody *ever* tells me what's going on.

Wrong: I hardly never get a chance to answer.
Right: I hardly *ever* get a chance to answer.

Wrong: They have*n't* done *nothing*.
Right: They have*n't* done *anything*.
Right: They have done *nothing*.

**d.** Do not use an adjective for an adverb.

Wrong: He is *sure* clever.
　　　　　　 adj.

Right: He is *surely* clever.
　　　　　　 adv.

**Easy Aid:** Substitute the adverb *very* for the problem modifier.

Wrong:   The movie is *real* scary.   (VERY scary? Yes.)
<br>adj.

Right:    The movie is *really* scary.
<br>adv.

*Very* works, so the adverb *really* is correct.

**e.** Don't use an adverb instead of an adjective after a **linking verb** (44-c).

Wrong:   This egg smells *badly*.
<br>adv.
Right:    This egg smells *bad*.
<br>adj.

Wrong:   The roast tastes *well*.
<br>adv.
Right:    The roast tastes *good*.
<br>adj.

**f.** Certain adjectives may be used instead of adverbs in *idiomatic* expressions: expressions that are acceptable because they have been used for a long time. For example, you might say to someone: "Come close." You would never say: "Come closely." Another familiar idiom is found in this expression: "Deer crossing. Drive slow."

**g.** Be sure that adverbs such as *only* and *just* are placed correctly. A change in placement can change the meaning of the sentence.

*Only she* participated in two committees.

(no one else did—only *she*)

She *only participated* in two committees.

(she participated; she didn't chair or take a leading role)

She participated in *only two* committees.

(not in three or four)

**h.** Avoid the **double comparison** error. To form the comparative degree of an adverb, add either "-er" or "more" to the adverb (62-b), but do not use both methods together. The same rule applies when forming the superlative degree (62-c). This "double comparison" principle is the same as 56-c.

> Wrong:  Jane drove *more faster* than Dick.
> Right:     Jane drove *faster* than Dick.

> Wrong:  Of the four contestants, Jane drove the *most fastest.*
> Right:     Of the four contestants, Jane drove the *fastest.*

# PREPOSITIONS

## 64. A JOINING WORD: THE PREPOSITION

**a.** A **preposition** is a word that shows the relationship between a noun or a pronoun and some other word in the sentence.

| went | *to* | school | called | *upon* | her |
|------|------|--------|--------|--------|-----|
| verb | prep. | noun | verb | prep. | pron. |

**b.** The noun or pronoun that follows a preposition is called the **object of the preposition.**

for a *dollar*          after *us*
    obj.                    obj.

on the *plane*          between *them* and *us*
    obj.                    (compound object)

## 65. PREPOSITIONAL PHRASES

A **prepositional phrase** includes the preposition, the object of the preposition, and modifiers of the object.

At the next corner, turn right.
    *phrase*

*at* = preposition
*corner* = object of the preposition
*the* and *next* modify *corner*

The baby crawled under the breakfast table.
    *phrase*

*under* = preposition
*table* = object of the preposition
*the* and *breakfast* modify *table*

## 66. FREQUENTLY USED PREPOSITIONS

**a.** A **simple preposition** is a one-word preposition. Here are the most often used prepositions.

| | | | |
|---|---|---|---|
| aboard | behind | in | throughout |
| about | below | inside | to |
| above | beneath | into | toward |
| across | beside | of | under |
| after | between | off | underneath |
| against | beyond | on | until |
| along | by | out | unto |
| among | down | outside | up |
| around | during | over | upon |
| as | except | pending | with |
| at | for | since | within |
| before | from | through | without |

**b.** A **phrasal preposition** is a preposition made up of two or more words.

*according to* my favorite weather forecaster
*because of* my preference for tigers
*due to* her star-studded past
*from across* the wild and stormy seas
*from among* the seven stalwart brothers
*from between* the two towering silver birches
*from under* the gaily-decorated dock
*in accordance with* your clear but unpleasant instructions
*in front of* the madly jeering crowd
*in place of* her original two-hour speech
*in spite of* his deep, unreasoning antagonism
*on account of* the Abominable Snowman
*out of* this century's most bitter election
*with regard to* your recent absurd proposal

## 67. THE PART OF SPEECH OF A WORD DEPENDS ON ITS USE IN A SENTENCE

Words that are ordinarily prepositions may sometimes be used as adverbs or conjunctions.

*preposition:*  We talked *before* dinner.

> *Before* shows the relationship between *dinner*, its object, and *talked*.

*adverb:*  We talked about this *before*.

> *Before* has no object in this sentence.
> *Before* modifies *talked*, a verb.
> *Before* is therefore a TIME adverb (59) answering the question ''when.''

*conjunction:*  We talked *before* we had dinner.

> *We talked* = an independent clause.
> *Before we had dinner* = a dependent clause.
> *Before*, a subordinate conjunction (72), connects the two clauses.

## 68. ADJECTIVE AND ADVERB PHRASES

**a.** Prepositional phrases are modifiers (8). A phrase that modifies a noun or a pronoun is called an **adjective phrase.**

> A book *in the hand* is worth two *in the library*.
> (''In the hand'' modifies *book*; ''in the library'' modifies *two*.)

> *With his carrot-red hair*, he knew he would be easily recognized.
> (The phrase modifies the pronoun *he*.)

> Swimming *at the beach* is my favorite pastime.
> (The phrase modifies the gerund [verbal noun] *swimming*.)

**b.** A phrase that modifies a verb, an adjective, or an adverb is an **adverb phrase.**

> The dictionary is the only place where success comes *before work.*
>
> > (The phrase modifies the verb *comes.*)
>
> Jacqueline, whistling *in the dark*, showed a special kind of courage.
>
> > (The phrase modifies the participle [verbal adjective] *whistling.*)
>
> Later *in the day* we visited the new mall.
>
> > (The phrase modifies the adverb *Later.*)

## 69. COMMON PREPOSITION ERRORS

**a.** Often a preposition is incorrectly tacked on to a word. Watch the following.

| WRONG | RIGHT |
|---|---|
| all of the girls | all the girls |
| blame on me | blame me |
| continue on with the work | continue with the work |
| cover over the desk | cover the desk |
| off of the table | off the table |
| out of the window | out the window |
| plan on a party | plan a party |
| remember of a song | remember a song |
| where at he went | where he went |
| where to he went | where he went |

**b.** *Without* is a preposition. Never use it in place of *unless* or *that*.

> Wrong: I never go to the circus without I think of my first visit.
>
> Right: I never go to the circus that I do not think of my first visit.
>
> or: I never go to the circus without thinking of my first visit.

> Wrong: Jake won't play without he can use his favorite bat.
>
> Right: Jake won't play unless he can use his favorite bat.
>
> or: Jake won't play without his favorite bat.

**c.** The object of a preposition may be a dependent clause (6-b). Confusion arises when the clause is introduced by *who* or any of its forms.

> Right: We have no information about *who caused the accident*.
>
>> (*Who* is not the object of the preposition *about* but the subject of its own clause; therefore, the nominative case is correct.)

> Right: Go camping with *whomever you wish*.
>
>> (*Whomever* is not the object of the preposition *with* but the object of its own clause.)

# CONJUNCTIONS

## 70. A CONNECTING WORD: THE CONJUNCTION

A **conjunction** is a word that connects words, phrases, or clauses. Conjunctions are classified as *coordinate* and *subordinate*. A coordinate conjunction connects sentence parts of equal importance, while a subordinate conjunction connects a less important part to a more important one.

## 71. COORDINATE CONJUNCTIONS

A **coordinate conjunction** connects (*a*) words, (*b*) phrases, or (*c*) clauses of equal structural rank. **And, but,** and **or** are coordinate conjunctions.

**a.** WORDS:

> *Mary* **and** *Martin* washed the dishes.
> > (The coordinate conjunction *and* connects two nouns.)

> Mary *washed* **and** *dried* the dishes.
> > (The coordinate conjunction *and* connects two verbs.)

**b.** PHRASES:

> I will meet you *at the bus stop* **or** *in Joe's restaurant.*
> > (The coordinate conjunction *or* connects two prepositional phrases.)

> I was asked *to write a quatrain* **and** *to read it in class.*
> > (The coordinate conjunction *and* connects two infinitive phrases.)

**c.** CLAUSES:

> *Luis trimmed the hedges,* **but** *he refused to mow the lawn.*
> > (The coordinate conjunction *but* connects two independent clauses (6-a).

*The Parts of Speech*

**147**

*The President does not desire another term of office,* **nor**
*would he accept a nomination.*

> (The coordinate conjunction *nor* connects two inde-
> pendent clauses.)

Note: These two sentences are examples of the compound
sentence (11-b).


## 72. SUBORDINATE CONJUNCTIONS

**a.** **A subordinate conjunction** connects a dependent clause with an
independent clause. (See 6, clauses.)

> Dinner will not be served until you are here.
>     *independent clause*        *dependent clause*

>> (*Until* is a subordinate conjunction that connects the
>> dependent clause with the independent clause.)

> Because the field was muddy, the game was canceled.
>     *dependent clause*        *independent clause*

>> (*Because* is a subordinate conjunction connecting the
>> dependent clause with the independent clause.)

Note: These two sentences are examples of the complex sentence (11-c).


**b.** Study these frequently used subordinate conjunctions. The relative
pronouns (30), are starred.

| | | |
|---|---|---|
| after | if | when |
| although | since | where |
| as | *that | wherever |
| as if | though | *which |
| because | unless | while |
| before | until | *who |
| except | *what | why |

## 73. CORRELATIVE CONJUNCTIONS

**Correlative conjunctions** are used in pairs.

| | |
|---|---|
| as much . . . as | not . . . but |
| both . . . and | not merely . . . but |
| either . . . or | not only . . . but |
| first . . . second | not only . . . but also |
| less . . . than | not so much . . . as |
| more . . . than | now . . . then |
| neither . . . nor | whether . . . or |

*Either* Martha *or* Louise will do the shopping.

Dick is *not only* our team captain *but also* our star quarterback.

Do you know *whether* Betty skates *or* skiis?

## 74. CONJUNCTIVE ADVERBS

**Conjunctive adverbs** are part conjunction and part adverb. A conjunctive adverb separates two independent clauses with the help of a semicolon. The following are conjunctive adverbs.

| | |
|---|---|
| consequently | moreover |
| furthermore | nevertheless |
| hence | on the other hand |
| however | therefore |

The film was boring; *consequently,* we left early.

Many homes were destroyed by the tornado; *however,* the Red Cross came to the aid of the homeless villagers.

Note: The above two sentences are examples of the compound sentence (11-b).

**Punctuation Aid:**

Notice that—most of the time—a comma is used after the conjunctive adverb.

> I studied day and night; therefore, I earned a high score on the SAT test.

> He is not, however, a promising candidate.

> She is a brilliant speaker; furthermore, she has an exciting and challenging program.

## 75. COMMON CONJUNCTION ERRORS

**a.** Use *and*, *but*, and *or* to connect expressions similar in structure. (See also parallel structure, 20).

> Wrong: She likes *to hike* and *swimming*. (connecting an infinitive and a gerund)
> Right:  She likes *to hike* and *to swim*. (connecting two infinitives)
> Right:  She likes *hiking* and *swimming*. (connecting two gerunds)

> Wrong: He enjoys *visiting* the various countries of Europe in the spring and *to study* their cultures. (connecting a gerund and an infinitive)
> Right:  He enjoys *visiting* the various countries of Europe in the spring and *studying* their cultures. (connecting two gerunds)

**b.** When a subordinate conjunction introduces two or more clauses of equal importance, the conjunction should be repeated before each clause.

> Wrong: She announced *that* she was going to France and her sister would take over the business.
> Right:  She announced *that* she was going to France and *that* her sister would take over the business.

**c.** Use the conjunction *than* (not *then*) after a comparative expression.

> Right: She was brighter *than* I thought.
> Right: Max was taller *than* Ellie.

**d.** If *say*, *think*, or *feel* is followed by an infinitive, use *that* before the infinitive.

> Wrong: Jacqueline thought to go back to school would be difficult.
> Right: Jacqueline thought *that* to go back to school would be difficult.

> Wrong: Philip said to go by boat would be more fun.
> Right: Philip said *that* to go by boat would be more fun.

**e.** Use *as . . . as* to express positive comparison.

> Wrong: Jill is clever *as* Marsha.
> Right: Jill is *as* clever *as* Marsha.

**f.** *Where* is a conjunction indicating place or position.

> Right: He is going to Chicago where he will take up residence.

Do not use *where* in place of *that*.

> Wrong: I read in an old almanac *where* mittens are merely gloves that are all thumbs!
> Right: I read in an old almanac *that* mittens are merely gloves that are all thumbs!

**g.** Use *so* to mean "with the result that."

> Right: She had studied hard, *so* she passed the test.

Use *so that* to express purpose.

> Wrong: She studied *so* she would pass the test.
> Right: She studied *so that* she would pass the test.

**h.** Do not confuse *when* and *than*. *When* follows "scarcely" and "hardly."

> Wrong: She had hardly been seated *than* the main speaker began.
> Right: She had hardly been seated *when* the main speaker began.

# INTERJECTIONS

## 76. AN EXPLOSION OF THE MIND: THE INTERJECTION

An **interjection** is a word thrown into a sentence to show surprise or strong feeling. Some common interjections are *oh! ah! ouch! wow!*

> *Oh*! The tire is flat.
> *Ouch*! That hurts.

Any other part of speech—noun, adjective, adverb, etc.—may be used as an interjection.

> *Good*! I like that.
> "*Fire!*" she shouted.

**Punctuation:** An *exclamation point* (229) is placed at the end of an interjection, followed by a capital letter—if the interjection shows *strong* feeling. However, if the exclamation is *mild*, a comma is used at the end of the interjection, followed by a small letter.

> *No*! He did not reveal your secret.
> *Well*, look who's here.

# SECTION IV

# Problem Words and Expressions

---

*Continued on Following Page*

153

## 77. ACCEPT—EXCEPT

  . . . **accept:**   verb meaning "to take," "to agree to"

         I *accept* your payment.

  . . . **except:**   preposition meaning "but," "not including"

         Everyone went *except* Jim.

## 78. ACCOMPANIED BY—ACCOMPANIED WITH

  . . . **accompanied by:**   Use with a person.

         Gina was *accompanied by* Max.

  . . . **accompanied with:**   Use with a thing.

         The hurricane winds were *accompanied with* hail.

## 79. ADAPT—ADOPT

  . . . **adapt:**   to adjust to a new situation; to change

         You must try to *adapt* to country living.

  . . . **adopt:**   to choose and accept without change

         If you *adopt* our customs, you will soon find yourself at ease.

## 80. ADVICE—ADVISE

  . . . **advice:**   noun meaning "opinion given as to how to handle a situation"

         The UN gave this *advice*: handle China with care and don't devour Turkey.

  . . . **advise:**   verb meaning "to give advice to"

         The UN will *advise* its members to handle China with care and not to devour Turkey.

## 81. AFFECT—EFFECT

... **affect:**    verb meaning "to alter," "to change"
      This new law *affects* my tax payment.

... **effect:**    noun meaning "result"
      The *effect* of the law is that my taxes will rise.

... **effect:**    verb meaning "to bring about"
      This new law will *effect* a tax change.

## 82. AGGRAVATE—IRRITATE

... **aggravate:**    verb meaning "to make worse"; usually used with things
      Your antagonism is only *aggravating* the problem.

... **irritate:**    verb meaning "to provoke," "to annoy"; often used with people
      Your constant tardiness *irritates* your parents.

## 83. AGREE TO—AGREE WITH

... **agree to:**    Use with a thing.
      We *agree to* the plan to list rattlesnake on the menu as "prairie eel."

... **agree with:**    Use with a person.
      Justin *agrees with* the food critic who claims that canned rattlesnake and rattlesnake soup are becoming popular in the U.S.

## 84. AIN'T

... Always incorrect; use "isn't" or "aren't."
      Wrong: It *ain't* so.
      Right:   It *isn't* so.

      Wrong: They *ain't* here.
      Right:   They *aren't* here.

## 85. ALL—ALL OF

. . . Use **all of** only with pronouns.

> *All of us* are going.
> *All of them* passed the test.

. . . Use **all** with nouns.

> *All the girls* are going.
> *All the students* passed the test.

## 86. ALL TOGETHER—ALTOGETHER

. . . **all together:**   all at one time, usually used in a physical sense

> We were *all together* at the optician's office when we saw the sign: EYES EXAMINED WHILE YOU WAIT!

. . . **altogether:**   entirely, completely

> Lena was *altogether* happy.

## 87. ALLUSION—ILLUSION

. . . **allusion:**   indirect reference to

> Millie made an *allusion* to the Greek god Zeus.

. . . **illusion:**   a hallucination; a false perception

> That the trees appeared blue was only an *illusion* caused by the mingling of light and shadow.

## 88. ALMOST—MOST

. . . **almost:**   an adverb meaning "nearly"

> *Almost* all winter sports are characterized by settings of ice, snow, and bones!

. . . **most:**   a pronoun or an adjective meaning "more than half"

> *Most* winter sports are characterized by settings of ice, snow, and bones!

## 89. ALOT—A LOT—LOTS

. . . **alot:**   always wrong

> Wrong:   *Alot* of people think Easter Sunday is Decoration Day!
>
> Right:   Many people think Easter Sunday is Decoration Day!

. . . **A lot** and **lots** are correct for "parcels of land." As slang, these terms are acceptable in speech but not in writing.

> Wrong:   She bought *a lot* of candy.
>
> Right:   She bought a *good deal* of candy.
>
> or:   She bought *much* candy.

## 90. ALREADY—ALL READY

. . . **already:**   adverb expressing by or before a certain time

> The train had *already* left.
>
> If you can substitute "by now," *already* is correct.
>
> The train had (by now) left.

. . . **all ready:**   adjective phrase expressing complete readiness

> We were *all ready* for the trip.
>
> If you can substitute "completely" for "all," *all ready* is correct.
>
> We were (completely) ready for the trip.

## 91. ALRIGHT—ALL RIGHT

. . . **alright:**   never correct

. . . **all right:**   meaning "everything correct"

> The proposed plan was *all right*.

## 92. AMONG—BETWEEN

. . . **among:** Use when discussing three or more persons or things.

Mom divided the pie *among* Alex, Matt, and me.

. . . **between:** Use when discussing two persons or things.

Mom divided the pie *between* Alex and me.

## 93. AMOUNT—NUMBER

. . . **amount:** for bulk items that cannot be counted: spinach, money, anger, friendship, squash

He asked for a small *amount* of maple syrup.

. . . **number:** for individual items that can be counted: dollars, eggs, potatoes, friends, walnuts

He learned that a large *number* of "syrup" trees are 200 to 300 years old.

## 94. ANGEL—ANGLE

. . . **angel:** a heavenly creature; someone as good as an angel

Kim said the two children were absolute *angels*, and she would be happy to take care of them at another time.

. . . **angle:** a figure made by two lines extending from the same point; a point of view

His *angle* in his speech is that children should be heard as well as seen.

## 95. ANGRY—MAD

. . . **angry:** strongly annoyed

The teacher was *angry* with Jeff.

. . . **mad:** crazy; insane

The *mad* dog bayed at the moon.

*Problem Words and Expressions*

## 96. ANGRY AT—ANGRY WITH—ANGRY ABOUT

. . . **angry at:** Use with an animal.

Sheila was *angry at* the hamster.

. . . **angry with:** Use with a person.

Max was *angry with* his sister.

. . . **angry about:** Use with a situation.

Max was *angry about* the situation in Asia.

## 97. ANXIOUS—EAGER

. . . **anxious:** to be worried about something

Jill was *anxious* about the expedition on Mt. Everest.

. . . **eager:** to look forward to; having a keen desire

Jill was *eager* to join the expedition.

## 98. ANYONE—ANY ONE

. . . **anyone:** indefinite pronoun meaning "any person; anybody"

Never argue with *anyone*: the other fellow has a right to his own idiotic ideas!

. . . **any one:** adjective–pronoun combination meaning "any single person or single thing"

*Any one* of the members is eligible.
*Any one* of the plans is acceptable.

## 99. ARRIVE IN—ARRIVE AT

. . . **arrive in:** Use with a city or town.

Darryl *arrived in* New Orleans on Tuesday morning.

. . . **arrive at:** Use with a small area.

Darryl *arrived at* the ballfield on Tuesday morning.

## 100. ASCENT—ASSENT

. . . **ascent:** the act of rising; an upward slope

The *ascent* of Mt. Everest is a challenge.

. . . **assent:** to agree to

Jack gave his *assent* to Syl's proposal.

## 101. AT (an unnecessary word)

. . . Do not use unnecessarily with ''where.''

Wrong: *Where* is the pen *at?*

Right: *Where* is the pen?

## 102. AWHILE—A WHILE

. . . **awhile:** adverb

Stay *awhile.*

. . . **a while:** article plus noun; use as object of the preposition ''for''

Rest *for a while* before you go out.

## 103. BAD—BADLY

. . . **bad:** predicate adjective meaning ''ill''

I felt *bad.* (meaning ''I felt ill.'')

. . . **bad:** predicate adjective used to express sorrow or regret

I felt *bad* when they agreed that the future isn't what it used to be.

. . . **badly:** adverb meaning ''very much''

The driveway is *badly* in need of repairs.
She wanted *badly* to win first prize.

### 104. BECAUSE OF—DUE TO

. . . **because of:** adverb phrase modifying a verb, adjective, or another adverb

Wrong: She was absent due to illness.

Right: She was absent *because of* illness.
(modifies the adjective "absent")

Wrong: He yelled due to the pain.

Right: He yelled *because of* the pain.
(modifies the verb "yelled")

. . . **due to:** adjective phrase modifying a noun or acting as a predicate adjective

Wrong: Her absence, because of illness, was recorded.

Right: Her absence, *due to* illness, was recorded.
(modifies the noun "absence")

Wrong: Her absence was because of illness.

Right: Her absence was *due to* illness.
(refers to the noun "absence")

### 105. BEING THAT or BEING AS—change to BECAUSE or SINCE

. . . **Being that** and **being as** are colloquial and should not be used in writing.

Wrong: *Being that* they live in clocks, cuckoos never have nests!

Right: *Since* they live in clocks, cuckoos never have nests!

Wrong: *Being as* you are unhappy, I'll forgive you.

Right: *Because* you are unhappy, I'll forgive you.

## 106. BESIDE—BESIDES

. . . **beside:**  preposition meaning "by the side of"

Work *beside* me.

. . . **besides:**  preposition meaning "in addition to"

*Besides* Koko, only Anne stood by me during the trial.

## 107. BORN—BORNE

. . . **born:**  past tense of **bear**, meaning "bring forth by birth"

Abel was *born* at 1 a.m. on July 4th.

. . . **borne:**  present perfect tense of **bear**, meaning "carry"

Charles has *borne* his brother's dishonesty for thirty years.

## 108. BREATH—BREATHE

. . . **breath:**  a noun meaning a "portion of air"

Maria took a deep *breath* before diving.

. . . **breathe:**  a verb meaning "to inhale some air"

Under water, a human being cannot *breathe* without help.

## 109. BRING—TAKE

. . . **bring:**  indicates movement *toward* the speaker

Ms. John said, "Please *bring* your test papers to me."

. . . **take:**  indicates movement *away from* the speaker

Ms. John said, "Please *take* this note to the office."

## 110. CAN—MAY

. . . **can:**    suggests ability

I *can* jog for five miles without stopping. (I have the ability to . . . )

. . . **may:**    suggests permission

Mother says I *may* jog after I have finished the dishes. (I have permission to . . . )

## 111. CANNOT

. . . **cannot:**    Always spelled as one word.

Wrong: Insects *can not* close their eyes.

Right:   Insects *cannot* close their eyes.

Exception: When "can" is followed by "not only," "can" and "not" are *not* linked.

Right: A bee can not only flap its wings 18,000 times in one minute but can also carry more than 300 times its own weight.

## 112. CANVAS—CANVASS

. . . **canvas:**    (noun) a type of closely woven fabric

The tent was made of *canvas*.

. . . **canvass:**    (verb) to ask for orders or political support

Lou *canvassed* the neighborhood to acquire additional support for his candidate.

## 113. CAPITAL—CAPITOL

. . . **capital:**    main; wealth; seat of government

(1) The *capital* reason for his success is his willingness to work hard.

(2) He invested his *capital* in the bank so that it would earn interest.

(3) The letter "E" is like London because it is the *capital* in England!

. . . **Capitol:**    (capitalized) the building in which Congress meets

The difference between America's *Capitol* and America's *capital* is that the first is in Washington and the second is in the stock market!

### 114. CITE—SIGHT—SITE

... **cite:**  to quote; to state (Must be followed by a noun.)

Wilson *cited*, as proof, Arthur's confession.

... **sight:**  to see (verb) or something seen (noun)

Bart *sighted* the comet at 3 a.m.

The most poignant *sight* in Washington, D.C., is the Vietnam Memorial.

... **site:**  location

We chose that *site* because of the many silver birches.

### 115. COMPARE TO—COMPARE WITH

... **compare to:**  used to point out similarities between two quite different things

Inflation can be *compared to* an automobile without brakes.

*Compare* Jenny *to* a peach, and you will see what I mean about her having a lovely complexion.

... **compare with:**  used to point out similarities and differences between two objects or persons

This house *compares* favorably *with* our old one.

*Compare* Jenny *with* Jeanie, and you will see why I thought they were sisters.

### 116. COMPLEMENT—COMPLIMENT

... **complement:**  that which completes

This red scarf is the perfect *complement* for a basically black outfit.

... **compliment:**  praise

*Compliments* are like perfume—meant to be inhaled, not swallowed!

## 117. CONCUR WITH—CONCUR IN—CONCUR TO

. . . **concur with:**   Use with persons. ("concur"—to act together to a common end; to agree)

He *concurred with* the rest of the committee about the best solution.

. . . **concur in:**   Use to suggest joint action.

She *concurred in* the plan to eliminate littering.

. . . **concur to:**   Use "concur" with an infinitive.

He *concurred to* prevent the opposition party from being successful.

## 118. CONTINUAL—CONTINUOUS

. . . **continual:**   repeated, but with interruptions

Jane's *continual* questions bothered me.

. . . **continuous:**   constant, with no interruptions

The fire alarm bell rang *continuously* for five minutes.

## 119. COULD OF—MAY OF—MIGHT OF—MUST OF—SHOULD OF—WOULD OF

. . . **could of:**   Always incorrect; use "could have."

You *could have* told me that a porcupine has 30,000 quills.

They *must have* known that a flying fox is really a bat that glides.

"Of" is a preposition and cannot be used as a helping (auxiliary) verb. "Have" is the correct auxiliary to form the verb phrases above.

## 120. COUNCIL—COUNSEL

. . . **council:**   (noun) a committee; a local governing body

We went to the Student *Council* for help.

. . . **counsel:**   (noun) advice

We went to the Student Council for *counsel*.

. . . **counsel:**   (verb) to give advice

He *counseled* them to avoid reckless behavior.

## 121. DESERT—DESSERT

. . . **desert:**   (accent on first syllable) noun meaning "arid land"

The camel is sometimes called the ship of the *desert*.

. . . **desert:**   (accent on second syllable) verb meaning "to abandon"

Rats *desert* a sinking ship.

. . . **dessert:**   (accent on second syllable) noun meaning "a sweet course served at the end of a meal"

We had ice cream for *dessert*.

## 122. DIE OF—DIE FROM—DIE BY

. . . **die of:**   He *died of* tuberculosis.

. . . **die from:**   He *died from* exposure.

. . . **die by:**   He *died by* violence.

## 123. DIFFER FROM—DIFFERENT FROM—DIFFERENTLY FROM

. . . Use **from** after **differ**, **different**, or **differently**—not "than."

Wrong:   His homework is *different than* mine.
Right:    His homework is *different from* mine.

Wrong:   His homework *differs than* mine.
Right:    His homework *differs from* mine.

## 124. DIFFER FROM—DIFFER WITH

**. . . differ from:** Use to indicate a difference between persons or things.

My freezer *differs from* yours in that mine is larger and is self-defrosting.

**. . . differ with:** Use to indicate a difference of opinion.

He *differed with* me about who should receive the award.

## 125. DISINTERESTED—UNINTERESTED

**. . . disinterested:** impartial, not biased

Jack can make the decision; he is a *disinterested* observer.

**. . . uninterested:** not interested at all

Jack is *uninterested* in checkers and never plays at all.

## 126. DONE

**. . . done:** Use only with "have," "has," or "had."

**Done** is the past participle of **do** (do, did, done). See 41-d.

Wrong: Bill *done* his homework.
Right: Bill *did* his homework. (past tense)
or: Bill *has done* his homework. (present perfect)
or: Bill *had done* his homework. (past perfect)

### 127. DON'T—DOESN'T

. . . **don't:** contraction meaning "do not"; use with all persons except third person, singular

> *I don't* enjoy large parties. (1st person)
> *You don't* have to shout. (2nd person)
> *They don't* plant tomatoes or beans. (3rd person, plural)
>
> *Not*: He, she, or it don't. (3rd person, singular)

. . . **doesn't:** contraction meaning "does not"; use only with third person, singular

> *Jim doesn't* want to go to the party.
> *It doesn't* make sense to do it that way.
>
> *Not*: I, you, we, or they doesn't.

### 128. EACH OTHER—ONE ANOTHER

. . . **each other:** Use when only two people are involved.

> Jack and Mindy talked with *each other*.

. . . **one another:** Use when more than two people are involved.

> Jack, Mindy, and Tom talked with *one another*.

### 129. ELIGIBLE—ILLEGIBLE

. . . **eligible:** qualified to be chosen; worthy to be chosen

> She is *eligible* to enter the contest.
> He is an *eligible* young bachelor.

. . . **illegible:** not legible; not readable

> Since his handwriting is *illegible*, his teacher cannot grade his essay.

## 130. EMIGRANT—IMMIGRANT; MIGRATE—MIGRANT

. . . **emigrant:** one who leaves one country in order to live in another

> Several boatloads of *emigrants* from South Korea set sail for the U.S.

. . . **immigrant:** one who enters a new country with the intention of taking up permanent residence

> Antonia, who was born in Poland, is a recent *immigrant*.

. . . **migrate:** to travel from one place to another

> Every February the gray whales *migrate* from the Bering Sea to the Mexican coast.

. . . **migrant:** a farm laborer who moves from place to place to harvest crops

> After several long, hungry days, the *migrants* found temporary work in San Diego, California.

## 131. EMINENT—IMMINENT

. . . **eminent:** well-known; famous

> An *eminent* teacher once told me that a book shut tight is only a block of paper.

. . . **imminent:** threatening in the immediate future

> We could tell by the black clouds that a storm was *imminent*.

## 132. ENVELOP—ENVELOPE

. . . **envelop:** (accent on second syllable) a verb meaning "to wrap"
> *Envelop* the baby in this blanket.

. . . **envelope:** (accent on first syllable) a noun meaning "a flat, paper container for a letter"
> He placed the valentine in the *envelope* and mailed it.

*Laugh Your Way Through Grammar*

## 133. EVERYDAY—EVERY DAY

. . . **everyday:** an adjective meaning "common," "usual"

Jumping from helicopters is an *everyday* experience for him.

. . . **every day:** an adjective-noun combination meaning "day after day"

Her son does his homework *every day*.

## 134. EVERYONE—EVERY ONE

. . . **everyone:** indefinite pronoun that always refers to a person

*Everyone* knows that an intersection is the meeting place of headlights and light heads!

. . . **every one:** adjective-pronoun combination that can refer to a person or a thing

*Every one* of the psychiatrists agreed that a person with inhibitions is tied up in "nots"!

*Every one* of the flowers at the entrance to Disneyland is replaced seven times a year.

## 135. FARTHER—FURTHER

. . . **farther:** measures physical distance only

My house is five miles *farther* from school than your house is.

. . . **further:** measures non-physical distance

Jim is *further* in his studies than Max.

## 136. FEWER—LESS

. . . **fewer:** modifies a noun that can be counted

A human has *fewer* wisdom teeth than an elephant. (A human has four; an elephant has 24!)

. . . **less:** modifies a noun that can't be counted

But the elephant has *less* wisdom than a human—probably!

### 137. FIRSTLY

. . . Avoid using **firstly** at all. Use "first."

### 138. FORMALLY—FORMERLY

. . . **formally:**  established by custom or rule

For the prom, he was *formally* dressed in a tuxedo.

She was *formally* addressed as president by the members of the committee.

. . . **formerly:**  earlier in time

This man, *formerly* called Sam Smith, is now known as Sam Spade.

### 139. -FUL—FULL

. . . **-ful:**  the correct adjective ending
beauti*ful*—merci*ful*—bounti*ful*

. . . **full:**  used only as a separate word
Jackie is *full* of ideas.
That box is *full* of junk.

### 140. GONE

. . . **gone:**  Use only with "have," "has," or "had."

**Gone** is the past participle of **go** (go, went, gone).

Wrong: José *gone* to the store.
Right:  José *went* to the store. (past tense)
or:  José *has gone* to the store. (present perfect)
or:  José *had gone* to the store. (past perfect)

### 141. GOOD—WELL

. . . **good:**  always an adjective
Isabel is a *good* skater.
Isabel looks *good*. (meaning "attractive")
Isabel feels *good*. (meaning "happy")

... **well:**  usually an adverb, but an adjective when it is used to refer to health

> Isabel skates *well*. (adverb)
> Isabel feels *well*. (adjective, describing her health)

> Note:  She is *good*.  (has a good nature, is moral)
> She is *well*.  (is healthy)

Both sentences are correct, but they have different meanings.

## 142. GORILLA—GUERRILLA

... **gorilla:**  noun meaning "an anthropoid ape"

> Tarzan chatted with the *gorillas* in the trees.

... **guerrilla:**  noun or adjective referring to one who engages in irregular warfare

> The secret activities of the *guerrillas* were hampered by the curiosity of the friendly *gorillas*.

## 143. GOT

... **got:**  Do not use unnecessarily with "have," "has," or "had."

> Wrong:  The aardvark *has got* a sticky tongue that is a foot and a half long.
> Right:  The aardvark *has* a sticky tongue that is a foot and a half long.

> Wrong:  They *have got* a new definition for violinist: someone up to the chin in music.
> Right:  They *have* a new definition for violinist: someone up to the chin in music.

### 144. GRADUATE—GRADUATE FROM

. . . If the verb **graduate** precedes the name of an institution, the preposition **from** must be used.

Wrong: Jesse *graduated* Merrydale High School in 1988.

Right: Jesse *graduated from* Merrydale High School in 1988.

Wrong: After *graduating* Merrydale High School, Jesse joined the Marines.

Right: After *graduating from* Merrydale High School, Jesse joined the Marines.

### 145. HAD OUGHT

. . . **had ought:** Always incorrect.

Wrong: A grapefruit *had ought* to be described as a popular eye tonic.

Right: A grapefruit *ought* to be described as a popular eye tonic.

### 146. HANGED—HUNG

. . . **hanged:** used to describe the execution of a person

The murderer was *hanged* because he had committed a capital offense.

. . . **hung:** used to describe things that are suspended

The picture was *hung* on the north wall.
Mary *hung* her coat on the coatrack.

### 147. HEALTHY—HEALTHFUL

. . . **healthy:** indicates good physical condition
People are *healthy*.
Animals are *healthy*.

. . . **healthful:** indicates something that leads to good health
Spinach is a *healthful* food.
Exercise in moderation is *healthful*.

## 148. HISTORIC—HISTORICAL

. . . **historic:**    important as a part of history

The Capitol is a *historic* building.

Many *historic* landmarks are being preserved and even restored.

. . . **historical:**    based on a special period in history

John Jakes writes *historical* novels.

He collected the *historical* facts about the Boston Massacre before he developed his own theory as to its results.

## 149. HOPEFULLY

. . . **hopefully:**    an adverb meaning "in a hopeful manner"; it cannot mean "we hope" or "it is hoped"

Right:    Christine is working *hopefully* for a scholarship.

Wrong:    *Hopefully*, the two countries will not go to war.

Right:    It is *hoped* that the two countries will not go to war.

It is best not to use *hopefully* at all, since it is often used incorrectly.

## 150. IMPLY—INFER

. . . **imply:**    to hint; to suggest

When Zach said that about 17,000 distinctive smells have been classified, he was *implying* that he is an expert on odors.

. . . **infer:**    to conclude

When Zach said that about 17,000 distinctive smells have been classified, we *inferred* that he is an expert on odors.

## 151. IN—INTO

. . . **in:**    means "inside"

Bert is *in* the drawing room.

. . . **into:**    is used to indicate the act of "entering"

Bert is going *into* the drawing room.

## 152. INSIDE OF

. . . **inside of:**    Do not use **inside of** for **within**.

Wrong: She built the hut *inside of* a week.
Right:    She built the hut *within* a week.

. . . **inside of:**    Do not use **inside of** for **inside**.

Wrong: Stay *inside of* the amusement park.
Right:    Stay *inside* the amusement park.

## 153. IRREGARDLESS

. . . **irregardless:**    Always wrong.

Wrong: He went *irregardless* of his mother's warning.
Right:    He went *regardless* of his mother's warning.

## 154. IS BECAUSE, IS WHEN, IS WHERE, IS WHY

. . . Never use an adverbial clause after any form of the verb "to be."

Wrong: His anger *is because* he is suffering.
Right:    His anger is due to his suffering.
or:    He is angry because he is suffering.

Wrong: Inflation *is when* wallets are getting bigger and shopping bags are getting smaller.
Right:    Inflation is a time when wallets are getting bigger and shopping bags are getting smaller.
or:    Inflation usually means that wallets are getting bigger and shopping bags are getting smaller.

Wrong: Matt's Club *is where* the action is.
Right:  Matt's Club is the place where the action is.
or:  Matt's Club is the scene of the action.

Wrong: Politicians are often in hot water; *that's why* they sometimes get hardboiled!
Right:  Politicians are often in hot water; that's the reason they sometimes get hardboiled!
or:  Because politicians are often in hot water, they sometimes get hardboiled!

## 155. IT

. . . **It** must have an antecedent: a specific word to which **it** refers. Do not try to make **it** refer to an entire clause.

> Wrong: When you feel yourself turning green with envy, *it* means you're ripe for trouble.
> Right:  When you feel yourself turning green with envy, you're ripe for trouble.

## 156. KIND OF A, SORT OF A, TYPE OF A

. . . Do not use the article **a** or **an** after **kind of, sort of,** and **type of**.

> Wrong: What *kind of a* driver never gets arrested?
> Right:  What *kind of* driver never gets arrested? (a screwdriver)

## 157. KINDS

. . . The plural **kinds** must be used after "two" or more.

> Wrong: two *kind* of *oranges*
> Right:  two *kinds* of *oranges*
>
> Wrong: several *kind* of *oranges*
> Right:  several *kinds* of *oranges*

## 158. LATER—LATTER

. . . **later:** comparative form of the adjective **late**

Luis came late, but Jack came even *later*.

. . . **latter:** relating to the second of two persons or things

You can study in the morning or you can study now, but the *latter* is preferable.

## 159. LAY—LIE

. . . **lay:** means to place, to put; a transitive verb (always takes an object)

Principal parts: lay, laid, (have, has, had) laid

I *lay* the book on the table.
("book"—direct object)
Yesterday he *laid* the book on the table.
He *has laid* a book on the table every day this week.

(If you mentally replace each italicized verb with "put" and the sentence makes sense, then you know that some form of **lay** is the correct verb.)

. . . **lie:** means to recline, to stretch out; an intransitive verb (never takes an object)

Principal parts: lie, lay, (have, has, had) lain

He *lies* on the bed every day at two.
Yesterday she *lay* on the bed.
That book *has lain* on the table for three days.

## 160. LAYING—LYING

. . . **laying:** the present participle of **lay**

I am *laying* (putting, placing) the book on the table.

. . . **lying:** the present participle of **lie**

He is *lying* (reclining) on the bed.

*Laugh Your Way Through Grammar*

## 161. LEARN—TEACH

. . . **learn:**  to acquire information or a skill
I am *learning* Spanish.
I have *learned* to type.

. . . **teach:**  to impart or give information or a skill
My brother will *teach* me Spanish.
My brother *taught* me to type.

## 162. LEAVE—LET

. . . **leave:**  means "to go away"; "to abandon"
Please *leave* me now. (go away)

. . . **let:**  means "to allow"; "not to disturb"
Please *let* me alone. (don't disturb me)
Please *let* me write that story for the paper. (allow me to)

Notice that **let** functions as an *auxiliary* verb while **leave** never does. Hence . . .
*Let's go* to the game.    *Let* me walk alone.

## 163. LEND—LOAN—BORROW

. . . **lend:**  a verb meaning "to let someone have something on condition it be returned"
I promised to *lend* him $100.

. . . **loan:**  a noun meaning "something lent"
I obtained a *loan* of $100.

. . . **borrow:**  a verb meaning "to receive something with the understanding that one will return it"
I would like to *borrow* $100.

## 164. LIABLE—LIKELY

. . . **liable:**  expresses an unpleasant possibility
If you walk on ice, you are *liable* to fall.

. . . **likely:**  expresses possibility
Katrina is *likely* to be elected.

## 165. LIKE—AS—AS IF

. . . **like:** can be a preposition, but never a conjunction

Wrong: They are acting *as* children.
Right: They are acting *like children.*
  ("like children"—prepositional phrase)

Wrong: "Nobody can do it *like* McDonald's can."
Right: "Nobody can do it *as McDonald's can.*"
  ("as McDonald's can"—clause)

Wrong: She said it *like* she meant it.
Right: She said it *as if she meant it.*
  ("as if she meant it"—clause)

## 166. LOOSE—LOSE

. . . **loose:** adjective meaning "not tight"

"*Loose* lips sink ships!" (World War II slogan)

. . . **lose:** verb meaning "to misplace"

If you *lose* an hour in the morning, you will chase it all the day.

## 167. MAJORITY—PLURALITY

. . . **majority:** Means more than half. If **majority** refers to a specific number, it takes a singular verb.

Melanie's *majority was* three votes.

If **majority** refers to the individual members of a group, it takes a plural verb.

A *majority* of the team *are* going to Miami.

. . . **plurality:** Means more than anyone else received, but not necessarily more than half.

He won with a *plurality* of three votes.

Although she received a *plurality* of the votes cast, she did not receive the majority needed for election.

**180**

### 168. MAY—MIGHT

... **may:** expresses a possibility

I *may* go to college next fall.

... **might:** expresses a possibility but with more doubt

I *might* go to college next fall.

### 169. MAY BE—MAYBE

... **maybe:** adverb meaning "perhaps"

*Maybe* a compulsive golfer should be called a crackputt!

... **may be:** verb phrase

The abdomen *may be called* the Department of the Interior!

**Easy Aid:** If you're in doubt, substitute the word "perhaps." If it works, use "maybe" (one word); if it doesn't, use "may be" (two words).

### 170. MORAL—MORALE

... **moral:** noun or adjective indicating proper behavior

Sue's *moral* code prevented her from lying. ("moral"—adjective modifying "code")

Jamie's *morals* are based on the precept: "Do unto others as you would have others do unto you." ("morals"—noun, subject of "are based")

... **morale:** noun meaning "general attitude" and "outlook"

Jess' *morale* is high, and he has a good chance of winning the contest. ("morale"—noun, subject of "is")

## 171. NOT ONLY . . . BUT ALSO

. . . The **not only** phrase must form a parallel construction to the **but also** phrase: that is, if a *verb* follows **not only,** a *verb* must follow **but also;** if a *noun* follows **not only,** a *noun* must follow **but also.**

> Wrong: An octopus not only has eight legs but also blue blood.
>
> Right: An octopus not only has eight legs but also has blue blood.
>
> Right: An octopus has not only eight legs but also blue blood.

## 172. NOTORIOUS—FAMOUS

. . . **notorious:**   well-known in an unsavory way

> Al Capone was a *notorious* gangster.

. . . **famous:**   well-known in a favorable way

> The *famous* Albert Einstein was a mathematical genius.

## 173. NUMBERS

. . . Spell out all numbers from one through ninety-nine as well as other numbers written as one word; for example, hundred, thousand, etc. Use Arabic numerals for the others.

> I own *three* cats and *twenty* mice.
> There are 990,000 people who own *300* books.

See also 239, numbers.

## 174. PAIR

. . . **a pair:**   a noun meaning ''a single thing with two parts that are used together''; takes a singular verb

> A pair of scissors *is* lying on the table.

. . . **two pairs:**   takes a plural verb

> Two pairs of scissors *are* lying on the table.

. . . **A pair** (referring to two individuals) takes a plural verb.

The pair of them *are* going to Niagara Falls.

## 175. PART FROM—PART WITH

. . . **part from:**   Use with a person.

I hate to *part from* my cousin.

. . . **part with:**   Use with a thing.

I hate to *part with* my good-luck charm.

## 176. PASSED—PAST

. . . **passed:**   a verb meaning "went by"; "approved"

Gina *passed* that store every day for a month.
In 1457, in Scotland, a law was *passed* making it illegal to play golf.

. . . **past:**   a preposition, an adjective, an adverb, or a noun

(1) Ellie is *past* the age for playing with dolls.
(preposition; *age* its object)
(2) For the *past* few days, Ellie has been depressed.
(adjective; modifying *days*)
(3) Frank waved as he walked *past*.
(adverb; modifying *walked*)
(4) In the *past*, I sometimes worried about unimportant things.
(noun; object of the preposition *in*)

## 177. PEACE—PIECE

. . . **peace:**   a state of quiet; freedom from disturbance

During the past 4,000 years, there have been fewer than 300 years of *peace*.

. . . **piece:**   a part of a whole

"It's a *piece* of cake!" he said sweetly as he broke the world's dessert-eating record.

### 178. PERSONAL—PERSONNEL

... **personal:**  relating to a person; private

He bought the company for *personal* financial gain.

... **personnel:**  a body of persons employed by a particular firm; may take a singular or a plural verb

Our personnel *is* made up of former farmers.

Our personnel *are* voting today on rules governing retirement.

### 179. PRAY—PREY

... **pray:**  a verb meaning "to plead," "to entreat"

Kit *prayed* that she would be rescued.

... **prey:**  a verb meaning "to seize and devour"; "to injure"

The owl *preys* on small animals and birds.

... **prey:**  a noun meaning "an animal seized for food; a victim"

The eagle is a bird of *prey*.
(The eagle does the seizing.)

The rabbit is often *prey* to the owl.
(The rabbit is the victim.)

Zeke is a *prey* to his own greed.
(Zeke is the victim.)

### 180. PRINCIPAL—PRINCIPLE

... **principal:**  the head person or the major item

Make a PAL of your *princiPAL*.

The *princiPAL* reason for his failure is that he didn't study.

... **principle:**  a ruLE or a truth

He lives by the *principLE* that honesty is the best policy.

## 181. PROPHECY—PROPHESY

. . . **prophecy:**   (The "cy" ending is pronounced "see.") noun meaning "a prediction of something to come"

Kate's *prophecy*—that her happiness would last only one week—came true.

. . . **prophesy:**   (The "sy" ending is pronounced "sigh.") verb meaning "to predict something that is to come"

Did Kate *prophesy* the endless rain we've had?

Kate *prophesied* the endless rain we're now having.

## 182. QUIET—QUITE

. . . **quiet:**   without noise or motion

Half of wisdom is keeping *quiet* when you have nothing to say.

A *quiet* tongue makes no enemies.

. . . **quite:**   to a considerable extent

The family that chews gum together *quite* often sticks together!

Silly Suzy was *quite* certain that steel wool is the fleece from a hydraulic ram!

## 183. RAISE—RISE

. . . **raise:**   means "to lift higher"; a transitive verb (always takes an object)

Principal parts: raise, raised, (have, has, had) raised

Maxine *raises* the flag every day.

Maxine *raised* the flag in front of the school.

Maxine *has raised* the flag in front of the school every day for a month.

. . . **rise:**    means "to move upward"; an intransitive verb (never takes an object)

     Principal parts: rise, rose, (have, has, had) risen

       The sun *rises* at 6 a.m.

       Maxine *rose* from the chair and went to work.

       The boys *have risen* every day at 5 a.m.

## 184. REAL—REALLY

. . . **real:**    an adjective meaning "genuine"

       That is a *real* diamond.
       This is a *real* adventure.

. . . **really:**    an adverb meaning "truly" or "actually"

       I *really* don't know the answer.
       That is a *really* beautiful diamond.

## 185. in REGARD, in REGARDS TO

. . . When used with **in** or **with,** the singular form, **regard,** is always used.

     Wrong: I am writing *in regards to* your letter.
     Right:    I am writing *in regard to* your letter.

## 186. SEEN

. . . **seen:**    Use only with "have," "has," or "had."

     **Seen** is the past participle of **see** (see, saw, seen). See 41-d.

     Wrong: Norm *seen* this license plate: EZ2PLEZ.
     Right:    Norm *saw* this license plate: EZ2PLEZ. (past)
     or:      Norm *has seen* this license plate: EZ2PLEZ. (present perfect)
     or:      Norm *had seen* this license plate: EZ2PLEZ. (past perfect)

## 187. SET—SIT

. . . **set:** means "to place in position, to put down"; a transitive verb (always takes an object)

Principal parts: set, set, set
Please *set* the book on the table.

Exceptions: Idiomatic uses of **set:**
The sun *sets* in the west.
Do you think the cement *has set*?

. . . **sit:** means "to take a seated position"; an intransitive verb (never takes an object)

Principal parts: sit, sat, sat
Please *sit* down.
She *sat* in the new chair.

## 188. SLOW—SLOWLY

. . . **slow:** an adjective
He is a *slow* starter.

. . . **slowly:** an adverb
She walked *slowly* down the street.

Exception: Drive *slow*. (a permissible idiom)

## 189. SOME—SOMEWHAT

. . . Do not use **some** instead of **somewhat** as an adverb.
Wrong: Jake felt *some* better in the morning.
Right: Jake felt *somewhat* better in the morning.

(Note: If you can replace with **rather,** use **somewhat.**)

## 190. STATIONARY—STATIONERY

. . . **stationAry:** stAnding in one place
The desk is stationAry. (It can't be moved.)

. . . **stationEry:** pEns, pEncils, and other writing supplies
He went to the stationEry store to buy stationEry.

## 191. STAYED—STOOD

. . . Do not use **stood** when you mean **stayed.** (Note: If you can substitute **remained,** use **stayed.**)
Wrong:  She *stood* in bed.
Right:  She *stayed* in bed.

## 192. SURE—SURELY

. . . **sure:**  an adjective
He is *sure* that he will pass.
It is a *sure* thing.

. . . **surely:**  an adverb
Katrina is *surely* happy about the results.
They *surely* ski like experts.

## 193. SURE AND, TRY AND—SURE TO, TRY TO

. . . Do not use **sure and** and **try and.** Use **sure to** and **try to.**
Wrong:  Be *sure and* remind him that there has been only one indispensable man: Adam!
Right:  Be *sure to* remind him that there has been only one indispensable man: Adam!

Wrong:  Sheila told her husband she would *try and* buy a car with power steering for backseat drivers.
Right:  Sheila told her husband she would *try to* buy a car with power steering for backseat drivers.

## 194. THEIR—THERE—THEY'RE

. . . **their:**  possessive adjective
They lost *their* jackets.

. . . **there:**  adverb indicating place
He sat in the bleachers and left his jacket *there*.

. . . **they're:**  contraction meaning "they are"
*They're* sure that even Joshua couldn't make the modern "son" stand still!

## 195. THEN—THAN

. . . **then:** an adverb denoting time
He studied; *then* he went home.

. . . **than:** a conjunction suggesting comparison
It is better to wear out *than* to rust out.

## 196. THIS, THAT, THESE, THOSE with HERE or THERE

. . . Never use **here** or **there** after **this, that, these,** or **those.**

Wrong: this *here* tomato
Right: this tomato

Wrong: that *there* tomato
Right: that tomato

## 197. THIS, THAT, THESE, THOSE with KIND(s), SORT(s), TYPE(s)

. . . **this** and **that:** always singular
. . . **these** and **those:** always plural

Right: this (that) *kind* of *tomato* or *tomatoes*
Right: these (those) *kinds* of *tomatoes*

Right: this (that) *type* of *student*
Right: these (those) *types* of *students*

## 198. TO—TOO—TWO

. . . **to:** preposition; introduces a prepositional phrase
Three of every four visitors *to Walt Disney World* are adults.

. . . **too:** also; more than enough
A man is never *too* old to learn, but he is sometimes *too* young.

. . . **two:** the number 2
For every child who turns sixteen, *two* adults turn pale.

### 199. UP (an unnecessary word)

. . . Avoid using **up** unnecessarily.

> Wrong: Silly Suzy opened *up* a box of crackers to celebrate the Fourth of July.
> Right:  Silly Suzy opened a box of crackers to celebrate the Fourth of July.

> Wrong: Please close *up* the door.
> Right:  Please close the door.

> Wrong: They washed *up* the dishes.
> Right:  They washed the dishes.

### 200. USE TO—USED TO

. . . **Used to** is correct; **use to** is always incorrect.

> Wrong: She *use to* say that dieting is the triumph of mind over platter!
> Right:  She *used to* say that dieting is the triumph of mind over platter!

### 201. WANT

. . . Certain uses of **want** are incorrect although they are used often in speech.

> Wrong: She *wants for you* to be ambitious.
> Right:  She *wants you* to be ambitious.

> Wrong: She *wants you should be* ambitious.
> Right:  She *wants you to be* ambitious.

> Wrong: She wants *in*.
> Right:  She wants *to come in*.

> Wrong: She wants *out*.
> Right:  She wants *to go out*.

## 202. WEATHER—WHETHER

... **weather:**  condition of the atmosphere—heat or cold, rain or sun, etc.

> The one person who's always wrong yet never fired is the *weather* forecaster.

... **whether:**  usually used with ''or'' to express a choice of alternatives (the ''or'' may be implied or stated)

> I couldn't decide *whether* Europe *or* Africa would be my first choice for my vacation.

> I couldn't decide *whether* Europe would be my first choice for my vacation.

## 203. WHO (WHOM)—WHICH—THAT

... **who (whom):**  refers to a person

... **which:**  refers to an animal, or an inanimate object

... **that:**  refers to a person or to an inanimate object

> If a vegetarian is someone *who* (*that*) eats vegetables, what is a humanitarian?

> The roller coaster, *which* probably had its origin in the ice slides of 15th-century Russia, is a popular amusement park ride.

## 204. WHO'S—WHOSE

... **who's:**  a contraction meaning ''who is''

> Tim is the one *who's* insisting that an alarm clock is something that scares the daylight into you!

> *Who's* going to insist that the hen is immortal because her ''son'' never sets?

**. . . whose:**    a possessive pronoun

> *Whose* words are these: "Heavier-than-air flying machines are impossible"? (Lord Kelvin, in 1895)

**Easy Aid:** When in doubt, substitute "who is." If it works, use **who's.** If it doesn't, use **whose.**

**WHO (WHOM)—WHOSE.** For a further study, see 37-f.

## 205. YOU'RE—YOUR

**. . . you're:**    a contraction meaning "you are"

> If *you're* not afraid to face the music, you may someday lead the band.

**. . . your:**    a possessive adjective

> Do you have *your* checkbook with you?

**Easy Aid:** When in doubt, substitute "you are." If it works, use **you're.** If it doesn't, use **your.**

# SECTION V

## Capitalization, Punctuation, Spelling—And Other Matters

### CAPITALIZATION

### PUNCTUATION

---

*Continued on Following Page*

# CAPITALIZATION

**206.** Capitalize the pronoun **I** and the interjection **O,** but *not* the interjection **oh.**

> He said that I might go.
> "But O for the touch of a vanish'd hand . . . "
> "I'm happy, oh, so happy!" she cried.

**207.** Capitalize the first word of every sentence.

> The giraffe nibbled on the leaves.

**208.** Capitalize the first word of every line of poetry.

> "Is this a dagger which I see before me,
> The handle toward my hand? Come, let me clutch thee."

> Shakespeare—*Macbeth*

## 209. QUOTATIONS

**a.** Capitalize the first word of a direct quotation.

> He said, "The Grand Canyon is incredibly beautiful."

**b.** Do *not* capitalize the second half of a split quotation.

> "The Grand Canyon," he said, "is incredibly beautiful."

**c.** Do *not* capitalize a piece of a quotation.

> He used the words "incredibly beautiful" to describe the Grand Canyon.

**d.** Do *not* capitalize an indirect quotation.

> He said that the Grand Canyon is incredibly beautiful.

## 210. PROPER NOUNS AND PROPER ADJECTIVES

**a.** (1) Capitalize proper nouns and proper adjectives.

| PROPER NOUN | PROPER ADJECTIVE |
|---|---|
| Shakespeare | Shakespearean poetry |
| Ireland | Irish philosophy |
| France | French dressing |

(2) Capitalize the initials that are part of a proper noun.

J. P. Morgan
John D. Rockefeller

(3) Capitalize all nationalities, languages, and races.

Caucasian
Semitic
Belgian
Italian
Spanish

(4) Do *not* capitalize the prefix of a proper adjective.

anti-Russian
un-American
pro-French
pre-Columbian

**b.** Capitalize names of ships, trains, and planes.

the Mississippi Queen   (ship)
the Santa Fe Limited   (train)
Air Force One   (plane)

**c.** Capitalize historic events, periods, and documents.

| | |
|---|---|
| the Battle of Bunker Hill | the Twenties |
| the Bill of Rights | the Middle Ages |
| the War of 1812 | World War II |

**d.** Capitalize names of days, months, holidays, and calendar events.

| | |
|---|---|
| Tuesday | August |
| Fourth of July | Thanksgiving |
| Secretary's Week | Lent |

## 211. GEOGRAPHICAL TERMS

**a.** Capitalize geographical proper nouns.

| | |
|---|---|
| New York City | (but—the city of New York) |
| Mississippi River | (but—a river in Mississippi) |
| Warren County | (but—the county of Warren) |
| Pacific Ocean | (but—an ocean) |

Others: Boulder Dam; Fifth Avenue; Adirondack Mountains; Grand Canyon; Niagara Falls; North America; Lake Erie; the Dead Sea; the United States of America (Notice that "the" and "of" are not capitalized.)

**b.** Capitalize the first part of a hyphenated street-name—but *not the* second part.

Forty-second Street
Thirty-fourth Street

**c.** Do *not* capitalize points of the compass, but do capitalize these terms when they name parts of the country.

He traveled north on Route 1.
He lives in the North.

They drove southwest to Phoenix.
They settled in the Southwest.

Massachusetts is east of San Francisco.
Massachusetts is in the East; San Francisco is in the West.

## 212. ORGANIZATIONS

**a.** Capitalize names of all organizations and institutions.

| | |
|---|---|
| Sears, Roebuck & Company | Library of Congress |
| Boy Scouts of America | Lions Club |
| Chamber of Commerce | Photography Club |
| Democratic Party | Republican Party |

**b.** Capitalize words denoting members of an organization.

| | |
|---|---|
| the Boy Scouts | the Lions |
| the Democrats | the Republicans |

**c.** Capitalize brand names but *not* the common nouns that follow them.

| | |
|---|---|
| Ansco camera | Ford cars |
| Pillsbury biscuits | Johnson's baby powder |

## 213. EDUCATIONAL TERMS

**a.** Capitalize names of particular schools and colleges.

In Merrydale High School, the dictionary is the only place where success comes before work.
BUT: In our high school, the dictionary is the only place where success comes before work.

He attended the University of Texas in Austin.
BUT: He attended college in Austin, Texas.

**b.** Capitalize specific courses, usually numbered, and language courses.

She is studying Biology II this year. (numbered)
BUT: She is studying biology this year.

He is studying French this year.   (language)

*Laugh Your Way Through Grammar*

**c.** Do not capitalize names of classes.

> She is a senior.
> He is a sophomore.

## 214. RELIGIOUS TERMS

**a.** Capitalize names of religions whether used as nouns or adjectives.

| | |
|---|---|
| Protestant | the Protestant belief |
| Jewish | the Judaic law |
| Catholic | the Catholic creed |

Capitalize the names of religious congregations.

| | |
|---|---|
| Protestants | Catholics |
| Jews | Presbyterians |

**b.** Capitalize the word **God** and titles and pronouns that substitute for **God.** (Exception: do not capitalize the word "gods" when referring to ancient deities.)

> He studied the word of God daily.
> When God created the world, He did it in six days.
> He appealed to his Savior for help.

**c.** Capitalize the word **Bible** and all books of the Bible.

> She read the Bible daily.
> Her favorite book of the Bible was Genesis.
> She studied the Scriptures in college.

## 215. TITLES

**a.** Capitalize family titles when they are part of a name. Do *not* capitalize if a pronoun immediately precedes the title.

<blockquote>

That's Uncle Sam.

BUT: That is my uncle.

</blockquote>

<blockquote>

I asked Mother if I could go.

BUT: I asked my mother if I could go.

</blockquote>

<blockquote>

We visited Cousin Emma for one week.

BUT: We visited our cousin Emma for one week.

</blockquote>

**b.** Capitalize other titles when they are part of a name.

<blockquote>

I called Senator Smith about the problem.

BUT: I called my senator about the problem.

</blockquote>

<blockquote>

Dr. Joan Smith said that the only exercise some patients get is stretching the truth!

BUT: One doctor said that the only exercise some patients get is stretching the truth!

</blockquote>

<blockquote>

I know Judge O'Connor very well.

BUT: My friend is a judge on the Family Court.

</blockquote>

<blockquote>

He was the president of the senior class.

BUT: He was the President of the United States.

OR: He was President Ronald Reagan.

</blockquote>

(The word **president** when it refers to a President of a nation is always capitalized.)

Others: Mayor Carol Smith (but—the mayor of Merrydale)

Captain Fred Allen (but—a captain in the Air Force)

Principal Mike Trent (but—a principal of a school)

Note: *Vice President* is used when referring to the official of a nation; but—a student may be the *vice-president* of his class.

> He is an ex-President.  ("ex" not capitalized)
> She is Governor-elect.  ("elect" not capitalized)

**c.** Capitalize a title that takes the place of a name in direct address.

> Please understand, *Senator*, that procrastination is the fertilizer that makes difficulties grow!

> "Tell me, *Captain*, are we in immediate danger?"

## 216. PUBLICATIONS

**a.** In the names of magazines and newspapers, capitalize all words except articles, conjunctions, and prepositions unless the article is part of the name.

> *The New York Times*          *Sports Illustrated*

**b.** In the titles of books, poems, movies, works of art, etc., capitalize all words except articles, conjunctions, and prepositions unless one of these words begins the title. Exception: Prepositions of four or more letters are usually capitalized.

> *Of Human Bondage* (novel by Somerset Maugham)
> *A Tale of Two Cities* (novel by Charles Dickens)
> "The Star-Spangled Banner" (song by Francis Scott Key)
> "The Masque of the Red Death" (poem by E.A. Poe)
> *Woman With Book* (painting by P. Picasso)

## 217. OTHERS

**a.** After a colon, capitalize a long statement but not a short one.

> He didn't want to go: he had to study.
> He didn't want to go: He had an exam scheduled in three days, an important exam, and he had to pass it with a high grade if he hoped to be admitted to law school.

**b.** Capitalize the first word after ''Resolved.''

> Resolved, That the seniors will earn enough money to pay for a trip to Washington, D.C.

## 218. ABBREVIATIONS

Capitalize many—but not all—abbreviations.

**a.** Always capitalized:

> 2001 B.C.        A.D. 2001
> (Notice that **B.C.** follows the date,
> while **A.D.** precedes the date.)
> Jr. (Junior) as in John Smith, Jr.
> Sr. (Senior) as in John Smith, Sr.
> Vt. (Vermont), L.A. (Los Angeles)
> Feb. (February), Wed. (Wednesday)

**b.** Sometimes capitalized (optional):

> a.m. or A.M.        p.m. or P.M.

**c.** *Never* capitalized:

> v. or vs. (opposed to)        e.g. (for example)

(When in doubt, consult any dictionary.)

## 219. SALUTATION AND COMPLIMENTARY CLOSING OF LETTERS

**a.** Capitalize all important words of the salutation.

Dear Sir:                        My dear Madam:
Dear Mr. President:        Dear Ms. Edison: (or Mrs. or Miss)

**b.** Capitalize the first word of the complimentary closing.

Very truly yours,        Yours truly,
Sincerely yours,          Yours respectfully,

# PUNCTUATION

## 220. PERIOD

A **period** indicates a full stop.

**a.** A period is used at the end of every declarative and imperative sentence.

> A dietitian is someone who lives on the fat of the land. (declarative)
> Go home now. (imperative)

**b.** A period is used after most abbreviations and initials.

> T.S. Eliot      Pa. (Pennsylvania)
> Harry S. Truman      Dec. (December)

However, some often-used abbreviations are not followed by periods:

> UN (United Nations); FHA (Federal Housing Authority)

**c.** A period is placed inside end quotation marks.

> The speaker added, ''Humor is the hole that lets the sawdust out of a stuffed shirt.''

> Cyril Connolly called sculpture ''mud pies which endure.''

**d.** Three periods . . . (called an ellipsis mark) indicate the omission of some words of text. Use four periods if the ellipsis ends the sentence.

*Original quotation:* ''Nothing short of independence, it appears to me, can possibly do. A peace on other terms would, if I may be allowed the expression, be a peace of war.'' (George Washington)

*Shortened quotation:* ''Nothing short of independence . . . can possibly do. A peace on other terms would . . . be a peace of war.''

## 221. QUESTION MARK

A **question mark** is placed at the end of every question. It may also suggest doubt.

**a.** A question mark should be used at the end of a question.

> How can you take five strokes off your golf game? (Use an eraser!)
> What is a credit card? (A BUY pass!)

**b.** A question mark is used after a parenthetical question.

> When you study (you will, won't you?), remember to take detailed notes.

**c.** A question mark should be placed INSIDE the end quotation mark if it applies to the quotation only.

> I asked, "Why does she call her desk a wastebasket with drawers?"

BUT: A question mark should be placed OUTSIDE the end quotation mark if it applies to the whole sentence.

> Did you realize I was one of the "Terrible Thirteen"?

**d.** A question mark in parentheses (?) may be used to indicate uncertainty.

> Lea was born at 5 a.m. (?) last Sunday.

## 222. SEMICOLON

A **semicolon** indicates a strong pause.

**a.** A semicolon is used between two closely related independent clauses that are *not* connected by a conjunction.

> Don't tell a secret in the barn; horses carry "tails."
>
> Experience is a hard teacher; she tests first—and teaches afterward.

**b.** A semicolon is used between two independent clauses connected by a *conjunctive adverb* (74), or by an explanatory word or phrase.

| | | | |
|---|---|---|---|
| however | nevertheless | therefore | thus |
| for instance | otherwise | instead | hence |
| consequently | for example | then | so |

> Cross a turkey with a centipede; then everyone can have a drumstick!
>
> He was always at the foot of his class; consequently, he decided to become a chiropodist.

**c.** A semicolon is used for clarity if a sentence contains a number of commas.

> He invited Ellie, the class clown; Trudy, the class wit; and Tom, the class gadfly.
>
> We went to Paris, France, on July 1, 1988; and we returned to Los Angeles, California, on August 3, 1988.
>
> Jan requested a meeting with Tom Jones, the president; Claire Smith, the vice-president; Martin Gaylord, the secretary; and Charity Black, the treasurer.

## 223. COLON

A **colon** means—"Note what follows."

**a.** A colon is used to introduce a series following a noun or the phrase "as follows."

> Tessa invited three students: Jack Block, Sara Quentin, and Allan Pierce.

> Tessa invited the following students: Jack Block, Sara Quentin, and Allan Pierce.

However, the colon is *not* used following a verb.

> Wrong: Tessa invited: Jack, Sara, and Allan.
> Right:   Tessa invited Jack, Sara, and Allan.

**b.** A colon is used to introduce a word, phrase, or clause that explains the meaning of the main clause in a sentence.

> "Motel" is a portmanteau word: a blending of "motor" and "hotel."

> To remember the five Great Lakes, remember the word HOMES: H is for Lake Huron, O for Lake Ontario, M for Lake Michigan, E for Lake Erie, and S for Lake Superior.

In sentences of this type, a colon instead of a semicolon (222-a) may be used to separate the independent clauses.

> My father makes faces all day: he works in a clock factory!
> My father makes faces all day; he works in a clock factory!

When in doubt, use the semicolon.

**c.** A colon is used to introduce a quotation.

> Lincoln began his Gettysburg Address with these words: "Fourscore and seven years ago."

**d.** A colon is used after the salutation of a business letter.

> Dear Madam:          Dear Sir:
> Dear Mr. Edwards:    Dear Editor:

**e.** A colon is used—

 . . . between the hour and the minute.

  We left at 1:25 p.m.

 . . . between chapter and verse of the Bible.

  I read Genesis 1:4.
   (Book of Genesis, Chapter 1, Verse 4)


## 224. COMMA

A **comma** indicates a brief pause.

**a.** A comma is used after each noun in a series.

 Rosalic gave three examples of collective nouns: the dustpan, the garbage pail, and the vacuum cleaner.

**b.** A comma is used after each predicate in a series.

 Adam and Eve were good mathematicians: they added the devil, subtracted happiness, divided from God, and went forth to multiply.

**c.** (1) A comma is used after each adjective in a series.

 Clare Booth Luce once said that politicians talk themselves "red, white, and blue in the face"!

(2) A comma is used between *two* consecutive adjectives in a series IF the word "and" could be used, instead.

 Tabitha has a small, white kitten. (It is possible to say "small and white," so a comma is used.)

 Tabitha has a small Angora kitten. (It would be unnatural to say "small and Angora," so a comma is not used.)

**d.** A comma is used after each short clause in a series.

> Julius Caesar said, ''I came, I saw, I conquered.''
> The kitten played with the ball: she pushed it, she scuffed it, she tore it apart.

**e.** A comma is used after each phrase in a series IF each phrase starts with the same preposition.

> Bob often walks to the store, to school, and to church.

However—a comma is *not* used after phrases that do not start with the same preposition.

> Bob walked to the store on a chilly day in November.

**f.** A comma is used between the independent clauses in a compound sentence (11-b).

> I cracked the nuts, and Jim removed the meat.
> Tillie walked home, but Celia took the bus.

*Note:* A comma is *not* used between the parts of a compound predicate.

> Bryan says wealth is a disease, but he doesn't tell how to catch it. (comma—compound sentence)

BUT: Bryan says wealth is a disease but doesn't tell how to catch it. (no comma—compound predicate)

**g.** A comma is used after an introductory dependent clause in a complex sentence (11-c).

> If you split your sides laughing, you should run until you get a stitch in them.
> When the stars get hungry, they take a bite of the Milky Way.

**h.** A comma is often used after an introductory prepositional phrase.

> To the teenager, home is merely a filling station.

**i.** A comma is used after a verbal or verbal phrase that introduces a sentence.

> (1) Whistling, we walked down the street.   (participle)

> (2) Whistling merrily, we walked down the street. (participial phrase)

> (3) To perfect the process, we added a new acid. (infinitive phrase)

However—a verbal that is the subject of a sentence is *not* separated by a comma from its predicate.

> Eating is a pleasant social event.   (gerund as subject)

> "To err is human."   (infinitive as subject)

**j.** A comma is used before and after a verbal or verbal phrase that appears in the middle of a sentence.

> The six boys, whistling merrily, walked down the street. (participial phrase)

> The scientists, to perfect the process, added a new acid. (infinitive phrase)

**k.** A comma is often used before a verbal that appears at the end of a sentence.

> Walking down the street were six boys, whistling merrily.

**l.** Commas should be used to separate nonessential (non-restrictive) clauses or phrases from the rest of the sentence. Commas are *not* used with essential (restrictive) clauses and phrases.

> Jim Brown, who lives on Owen Avenue, won the election.

> > ("Who lives on Owen Avenue" is not essential to the meaning of the sentence and therefore is separated by commas.)

> The boy who lives on Owen Avenue won the election.

> > ("Who lives on Owen Avenue," identifying "boy," is essential to the meaning of the sentence and therefore is *not* separated by commas.)

> Sally, grinning happily, was declared the winner.
> (nonessential participial phrase)
> The girl grinning happily was declared the winner.
> (essential participial phrase)

**m.** A comma is used before and after an appositive within a sentence. If an appositive ends the sentence, only one comma is used. (See 19.) If an appositive is a single word, its connection is usually too close to require commas for separation.

> Amelia, a tall girl, went out for basketball.
> The favorite in the one-mile race was Jed, a runner with several awards.
> My sister Nancy is studying for the SAT.

**n.** A comma is used to set off words in direct address.

> Angela, please come here.
> Tell me, Mary, how you can carry water in a sieve. (Answer: first freeze the water!)

**o.** A comma is used after *yes, no, well, oh, why,* etc., at the beginning of a sentence. (See also 76.)

> Yes, I would like to receive a copy of your book.
> Well, perhaps I will go with you.
> Oh, he frightened me!
> Why, I hadn't even considered that possibility.

**p.** A comma is used before and after parenthetical expressions.

> A prison warden is a person who, not surprisingly, makes a living by the pen!
> "Old Blood and Guts" was, of course, a nickname for General George Patton.

**q.** A comma is used to separate items in dates and places.

> He was born in Akron, Ohio, on Tuesday, July 12, 1837.

In a ZIP code, a comma is used between the city and the state but is *not* used between the initials of the state and the ZIP number, as below.

> He sent the letter to his aunt in Radnor, PA 19088.

**r.** A comma is used to separate a quotation from the rest of the sentence.

> "Never lend money; it gives people amnesia," said Fred.

> Fred said, "Never lend money; it gives people amnesia."

In a broken quotation, the interrupter must be set off with two commas.

> "Never lend money," said Fred, "because it gives people amnesia."

However—do *not* use a comma with an indirect quotation.

> Fred said that we should go to the circus.

**s.** A comma is used WHENEVER NECESSARY to make the meaning clear.

> Wrong: Outside the moon glittered on the snow.
> Right:　Outside, the moon glittered on the snow.

> Wrong: If you want to study all night.
> Right:　If you want to, study all night.

> Wrong: To Charles Elizabeth is more mother than queen.
> Right:　To Charles, Elizabeth is more mother than queen.

**t.** A comma is used to indicate that a word has been omitted.

> Nina brought the spaghetti, and Jack, the sauce.

> Jane owns a goldfish; Millie, a guppy.

**u.** A comma is used after the salutation of a friendly letter.

> Dear Jack,　　　　　　　Dear Aunt Emily,

**v.** A comma is used after the complimentary closing of any letter, whether business or friendly.

> Love,　　　　　　　　Very truly yours,

> As ever,　　　　　　　Yours sincerely,

**w.** A comma is used before and after degrees and titles.

> Elizabeth Hunter, Ph.D., is speaking today.
> That is John L. Davis, Jr., on the speaker's platform.

**x.** A comma is never used to separate a subject from a predicate.

> Wrong: The storm with its high winds and pelting rain, destroyed the town beach.
> Right: The storm with its high winds and pelting rain destroyed the town beach.

## 225. QUOTATION MARKS

**a. Quotation marks** are used to indicate the actual speech of someone.

> "Excuse me while I disappear," said Frank Sinatra to some reporters.
>
> Frank Sinatra said to some reporters, "Excuse me while I disappear."
>
> "Excuse me," Frank Sinatra said to some reporters, "while I disappear."

When two sentences are quoted, the sentences may be punctuated in several ways.

> Jane said, "I hurt my knee. It's bleeding!"
>
> "I hurt my knee. It's bleeding!" Jane said.
>
> "I hurt my knee," Jane said. "It's bleeding!"
>
> "I hurt my knee," Jane said; "it's bleeding!"
>
> "I hurt my knee," Jane said, "and it's bleeding!"

Notice that the quotations are separated by commas from the rest of the sentence.

**b.** Quotation marks are used to emphasize a particular word or letter. Note: underlines may be used instead of quotation marks for letters.

> War knocks the "l" out of glory.
> She counted three "e's" in "cemetery."
> "Impossible" is an interesting word; most of it is possible.

**c.** Quotation marks are used around the titles of short literary works. Underline the titles of long literary works. (In print, underlines are italicized.)

> She read the poem, "The Raven," by Edgar Allan Poe.
> He read the novel, David Copperfield, by Charles Dickens.
> My favorite book is Guns of Burgoyne by Bruce Lancaster, and my favorite chapter in this novel is "The River."

**d.** Quotation marks are used with dialogue. Notice that a new paragraph is formed every time the point of view shifts from one speaker to another.

> "Come to my party," Sue urged.
> Tom nodded. "I'd like to." He grinned. "Masquerade parties are fun! Besides, how can I say 'no' to you, Sue?"
> "Good!" Sue's lips puckered with an impish smile. "See you at seven, then."

**e.** Single quotation marks are used to indicate a quotation within a quotation.

> "My favorite poem," said Tim, "is 'If' by Rudyard Kipling."

**f.** Quotation marks may be used with a long quotation, one that is two paragraphs or more. Quotation marks are used at the BEGINNING of each paragraph, but at the end of the LAST paragraph only.

However—the preferred treatment of a long quotation is to indent the entire quotation, to switch from double spacing to single spacing, and to omit quotation marks.

Lincoln's Address at Gettysburg in 1863 is memorable. Schoolchildren memorize it, Fourth of July orators quote it, and newspaper editors refer to it.

> Fourscore and seven years ago our fathers brought forth on this continent a new nation, conceived in liberty and dedicated to the proposition that all men are created equal.
> Now we are engaged in a great civil war, testing whether that nation or any nation so conceived and so dedicated can long endure . . .

Whenever possible, follow the indented style for extended prose quotations and for more than two lines of poetry.

**g.** Periods and commas are always placed INSIDE end quotation marks.

(1) Bert promised, "We're going hunting tomorrow."
(2) "We're going hunting," Bert promised, "tomorrow."

Question marks and exclamation points are placed INSIDE or OUTSIDE, depending on the sentence. (See 221-c, 229-b for additional examples.)

(3) Jay asked, "Can we go swimming tomorrow?" (The question mark goes with the question, inside the end quotation mark.)
(4) How do you spell "swimming"? (The question mark goes with the entire sentence, not with "swimming"; therefore the question mark goes outside the end quotation mark.)
(5) Jay asked, "How do you spell 'swimming'?" (The question mark is placed inside the double quotation mark, but outside the single quotation mark.)

## 226. APOSTROPHE

**a.** The **apostrophe** is used to indicate a missing letter or letters in a contraction.

| | |
|---|---|
| can't (cannot) | don't (do not) |
| haven't (have not) | isn't (is not) |
| o'clock (of the clock) | won't (will not) |

*Laugh Your Way Through Grammar*

It is also used to indicate the omission of letters or numbers in other expressions.

the Spirit of '76 (1776)
the Class of '89 (1989)

**b.** The apostrophe is used to create the plural form of numbers, letters, and words being discussed.

Jim wrote three ''6's'' on his paper.
There are two ''o's'' in ''kimono.''
Let there be no ''if's,'' ''and's,'' or ''but's''!

**c.** The apostrophe is used to form the possessive case of nouns. (See 24.)

**d.** The apostrophe is used to turn time and money nouns into possessive adjectives.

| | |
|---|---|
| a week's work | two weeks' work |
| a dollar's worth | two dollars' worth |
| a day's work | two days' work |

## 227. DASH

The **dash** is stronger than the comma, indicating a longer pause or interruption.

**a.** The dash is used to signal an interruption.

Carlos warned us that—oh, you aren't really interested!

**b.** Two dashes are used to separate a parenthetical expression from the rest of the sentence.

Jane said—and I'm sure she's right—that our final exam is tomorrow.

**c.** Two dashes are used to separate appositives that contain commas.

> Three entries—chicken legs, spare ribs, and pork shoulder— are favorites at the annual Orthopedists' Banquet.

**d.** The dash is used for emphasis.

> With only one leg, Lonny walked—yes, walked—over a hundred miles.

> Rain makes flowers grow—and taxicabs disappear!

**e.** A short dash is used to indicate the omission of the word "to."

> She studied from 4–6 p.m. every day. (4 *to* 6)

> For tomorrow, read pages 18–105. (18 *to* 105)

**f.** A dash is used before a summarizing statement.

> He stopped for a small snack—a bowl of clam chowder, a pizza, an ice-cream sundae, and three eclairs.

## 228. PARENTHESES

**a. Parentheses** are used to enclose a parenthetical expression.

> Jane said (and I agree with her) that money doesn't talk these days—it goes without saying!

> More boys than girls are colorblind (see accompanying chart), but parents are not always aware of this.

**b.** Parentheses are used to indicate that a complete sentence is parenthetical: not a necessary part of the text.

> You can find all kinds of information about bubble gum in your school library. (Check the card catalog, the vertical file, and *Readers' Guide to Periodical Literature*.)

## 229. EXCLAMATION POINT

**a.** The **exclamation point** is used after words or sentences showing strong feeling. (Also see 76.)

> Help!
> Help me! I'm drowning!
> How beautiful you are!
> There are thirty muscles in a cat's ear!

**b.** The exclamation point is placed inside or outside quotation marks, depending on the sentence.

> Lopez shouted, "I'm drowning!" (The exclamation point goes with the quotation, and therefore is *inside* the quotation mark.)
>
> I hate the sound of the word "kiosk"! (The exclamation goes with the whole sentence, not with the word in quotation marks, and therefore is *outside* the quotation mark.)

## 230. HYPHEN

**a.** A **hyphen** is used to combine two words into a compound adjective when the adjective precedes a noun.

> a well-turned phrase
> an ill-qualified clerk

However—when the two words follow the noun, a hyphen is not used.

> a phrase well turned
> a clerk ill qualified

**b.** A hyphen is used in numbers from twenty-one to ninety-nine.

**c.** A hyphen is used after "half" when "half" is used as a prefix.

> half-aware half-cocked half-dollar

**d.** A hyphen is used to divide a word at the end of a line of writing. The word should always be divided at the end of a syllable.

> Both he and his friend decided to invest mon-
> ey in Treasury bonds.

> You should be especially careful not to mis-
> spell the word "misspell."

NEVER place a hyphen at the beginning of a new line.

**231. UNDERLINING** (In print, this appears as italics.)

**a.** Underline the titles of long literary works, such as novels and biographies, and of movies and TV shows.

> Margaret Mitchell's novel, *Gone With the Wind*, was origi-
> nally called *Tomorrow Is Another Day*.

> In 1939 Ernest Vincent Wright wrote a novel, *Gadsby*, which
> had not a single "e" in it.

**b.** Underline the titles of magazines and newspapers (but not articles before these titles unless the article is part of the title.)

> She reads *The New York Times* every day.

> He reads *Sports Illustrated* regularly.

**c.** Underline the names of works of art, of ships, and of planes.

> Her favorite painting is *Toledo* by El Greco.

> He named his yacht *Annabel* after his mother.

> One of the most famous planes in the world is the *Spirit of
> St. Louis*.

# SPELLING

Most spelling rules have many exceptions, making them almost worthless. But a few have value. Here they are.

## 232. Prefixes

**a.** When adding a **prefix,** simply place it before the word. Retain the correct spelling of both word and prefix. For example: the word SPELL. Place the prefix before it—MIS. The correct spelling, then, is MISSPELL. Here are a few more examples.

> MIS + understood (MISunderstood)
>      + take (MIStake)
>
> IL + legal (ILlegal)
>     + legible (ILlegible)
>
> DIS + appoint (DISappoint)
>      + satisfy (DISsatisfy)
>
> IM + mediate (IMmediate)
>     + mature (IMmature)
>
> RE + commend (REcommend)
>     + hearse (REhearse)
>
> UN + usual (UNusual)
>      + necessary (UNnecessary)
>
> CO + operate (COoperate)
>     + ordinate (COordinate)
>
> PRE + paid (PREpaid)
>      + mature (PREmature)

**b.** Occasionally a hyphen is used after the prefix to prevent confusion. **Cooperate** is now accepted; so is **preempt.** But **copartner** may confuse, so it is usually written **co-partner.** When you are uncertain, check any good dictionary.

## 233. Suffixes

**a.** When adding a **suffix,** simply add it to the base word. Retain the correct spelling of both base word and suffix. For example: the word APPOINT. Add the suffix MENT for APPOINTMENT. Here are a few more examples.

> MENT + govern (governMENT)
>        + disappoint (disappointMENT)
>
> FUL + hope (hopeFUL)
>      + tear (tearFUL)
>
> ING + embarrass (embarrassING)
>      + cry (cryING)
>
> NESS + keen (keenNESS)
>       + cheerful (cheerfulNESS)
>
> LESS + care (careLESS)
>       + fear (fearLESS)
>
> *LY + final (finalLY)
>      + accidental (accidentalLY)
>      + critical (criticalLY)

*Note well:* Be sure to retain the ''-al'' when adding ''-ly'' to these adjectives.

**b.** If the suffix begins with a vowel and follows a silent ''e,'' drop the ''e.''

> hope + ing = HOPING
> guide + ance = GUIDANCE
> desire + able = DESIRABLE
> write + ing = WRITING

**c.** If the silent ''e'' follows a ''c'' or ''g,'' retain the ''e'' to keep the ''c'' or ''g'' soft.

> notice + able = NOTICEABLE
> change + able = CHANGEABLE
> courage + ous = COURAGEOUS
> peace + able = PEACEABLE

Exceptions: judgment; acknowledgment.

But: drop the "e" if the suffix begins with an "i" or "e."

> notice + ed = NOTICED
> notice + ing = NOTICING

**d.** If a word ends in a single consonant preceded by a single vowel, double the consonant when adding a suffix.

> occur + ed = OCCURRED
> plan + ing = PLANNING
> forget + ing = FORGETTING
> prefer + ed = PREFERRED

However—if the word is accented on the first syllable, do *not* double the consonant.

> profit + ed = PROFITED
> prefer + able = PREFERABLE
> benefit + ed = BENEFITED
> frighten + ing = FRIGHTENING

## 234. "EI"—"IE"

**a.** Start with the old rhyme:

> "i" before "e"
> except after "c"—
> or when sounded like "a"
> as in "neighbor" and "weigh."

**b.** The general rule is "i" before "e"—

> believe    fierce    thief    brief    wield

**c.** After "c," reverse the letters—

> receive    ceiling    deceive    conceit

**d.** When sounded like "a," reverse the letters—

> neighbor    weigh    freight    eight

Exceptions to (*b*): leisure, either, neither, height, veil, weird, seize, foreign.
Exception to (*c*): financier.

## 235. "Y" to "I"

**a.** If a word ends in "y" and the "y" is preceded by a consonant, change "y" to "i" when adding a suffix.

| | |
|---|---|
| try—tried | study—studies |
| lonely—loneliness | beauty—beautiful |
| crazy—crazily | marry—marriage |

Exceptions: dryness; shyness.

However—when adding "-ing," keep the "y."

| | |
|---|---|
| try—trying | marry—marrying |
| dry—drying | study—studying |

**b.** If the "y" is preceded by a vowel, keep the "y" when adding a suffix.

| | |
|---|---|
| enjoy—enjoyed | employ—employment |
| prey—preying | display—displayed |

Exceptions: day—daily; pay—paid; lay—laid.

## 236. WORDS ENDING IN "C"

If a word ends in "c," add a "k" before a suffix beginning with "e," "i," or "y."

picnic—picnicking—picnicked
mimic—mimicking—mimicked
panic—panicking—panicked—panicky

## 237. WORDS OFTEN MISSPELLED

absence
accidentally
accommodate
acquaintance
across
advertisement
again
aisle
allotted
all right

already
amateur
among
anonymous
appearance
Arctic
argument
arithmetic
article
assassinate

athlete
audience
aunt
author
automobile
autumn
auxiliary
avenue
awful
awkward

bachelor
banana
banquet
beauty
beginning
believe
benefited

bicycle
bookkeeping
business

busy
calendar
campaign
captain
cemetery
century
changeable
chaperon
character
chocolate

Christian
civilization
climate
clothes
cocoa
college
colonel
colossal
column
coming

commitment
committee
condemn
congratulate
conscience
conscientious
consensus
constitution
convenience
cooperate

cough
courageous
courteous

cousin
criticism
criticize
cruel
curiosity
curious
current

customer
daily
decision
defense
definitely
descendant
description
desirable
despair
desperate

develop
dictionary
difference
diploma
disappear
disappoint
discipline
disease
dissatisfied
doesn't

doubt
economical
ecstasy
eerie
efficient
eighth
electricity
eligible
embarrass
emphasize

encourage
engine
enough
equipment
equipped
especially
essential
executive
exercise
existence

extraordinary
familiar
famous
fascinating
fashionable
fault
favorite
February
feminine
fierce

figure
finally
financially
flies
foreign
fortunate
forty
fourth
freight
friend

fuel
garage
gazing
genealogy
generous
genius
genuine

geography
glorious
gnawing

government
governor
graffiti
grammar
grate
grateful
gratitude
great
grief
grocery

guarantee
guess
gymnasium
handkerchief
handsome
happened
happiness
harassed
harbor
haven't

height
heroes
hesitate
history
hoarse
honor
hoping
horizon
horrible
hospital

humorous
husband
hymn
idea
ignorant

imagine
imitation
immediately
impossible
independent

Indian
individual
industrial
influence
initial
inoculate
insurance
interpretation
interrupt
interview

irrelevant
irresistible
island
jealous
jewelry
journey
judgment
justice
kimono
kitchen

knit
knock
knowledge
laboratory
language
laugh
lawyer
legislature
leisure
length

lesson
liaison
library

license
lieutenant
lightning
liquid
literature
living
loneliness

losing
lovable
luxurious
magazine
maneuver
marriage
masquerade
material
matinee
mayor

meant
medal
medicine
medieval
minimum
minuscule
minute
mischievous
missile
misspell

mortgage
movable
musician
naive
necessary
nickel
ninety
ninth
noticeable
nuisance

occasionally

occurred
often
omitted
parallel
particularly
pastime
peddler
penicillin
permanent

perseverance
personally
picnicking
planning
pneumonia
possession
possible
prejudice
privilege
probably

procedure
professor
pronunciation
psychology
questionnaire
realize
receive
recognize
recommend
referred

repetition
restaurant
rhythm
roommate
sacrilegious
sandwich
satisfactorily
schedule
scissors
secretary

seize
separate
sergeant
shining
similar
sincerely
sophomore
souvenir
specimen
success

sufficient
supersede

surprise
syllable
tariff
temperature
theater
thoroughly
tragedy
transferred

treasurer
truly
twelfth

tyranny
ukulele
undoubtedly
unforgettable
unmistakable
unnecessary
until

vacuum
vegetable
vengeance
vicinity

villain
weird
wheat
wholly
width
worst

writing
written
yesterday
yield
yolk

# MNEMONIC AIDS

**238.** A **mnemonic aid** is any trick or clue that helps the memory. In spelling, mnemonic aids exist for many often-misspelled words.

For example: sepARATe is A RAT of a word. Once you have memorized this, you will never again misspell "separate."

Here is a short list of mnemonic aids. You may wish to create mnemonic aids for words that are a problem for you.

AGAIN   You will GAIN an A if you spell AGAIN correctly!

CEMETERY   Only "e's" are buried in a cEmEtEry.

CONSCIENCE   ConSCIENCE is not a matter of SCIENCE.

FEBRUARY   FeBRUary is a BRUtal month.

GRAMMAR   Don't MAR your gramMAR.

KIMONO   KIM and ONO wear KIMONOs.

LABORATORY   A LABORatory is a place where scientists LABOR.

LIBRARY   Spend time in a liBRAry and you will be a BRAin.

MEDIEVAL   It was easy to DIE in meDIEval times.

MINUSCULE   MINUS means less, so naturally there is a MINUS in MINUScule (which means "very small").

PIECE   Have a PIEce of PIE.

PRINCIPAL   A princiPAL is a PAL.

PRINCIPLE   A principLE of conduct is a ruLE.

SEPARATE   SepARATe is A RAT of a word.

VILLAIN   The VILLAin lives IN a VILLA.

# NUMBERS

**239.** **a.** Write out whole numbers from one through ninety-nine. Write out any of the above followed by hundred, thousand, etc. Hyphens are required for numbers twenty-one through ninety-nine.

> eighty-seven cents
> three thousand dinosaurs
> seventy-one million yo-yos

Exceptions: very large numbers are usually written with a combination of number and word.

> 71.3 million
> $21 billion

**b.** Use numbers when more than two or three words would be required.

> $1.87 (not—one dollar eighty-seven cents)
> 3,256 dinosaurs
> 71,498,232 yo-yos

**c.** Use numbers if several numbers are clustered.

> Volumes I through V contain 231, 300, 242, 311, and 400 pages, respectively.

**d.** Ordinal numbers follow the above rules.

> She struck out in the bottom half of the ninth inning.
> He ranked sixteenth in his class.
> He ranked 165th in his class.

**e.** Do not begin a sentence with a number.

> Three children came to the party.
> Nineteen eighty-eight was a Presidential election year.

**f.** Numbers referring to the same type of item within a sentence or a paragraph should be uniform.

> Jill owns 23 books, Willy owns 217, and Sally owns 3. (The second number, 217, must be written as a number, so the other two follow suit.)

**g.** Use numbers for dates and street numbers. Notice the use of commas.

> Rae lived at 36 Broad Street from September 9, 1980, to October 1, 1981.

> Her address is 25 Pine Street, Merrydale, Ohio  00067.

Write out particular centuries and decades.

> the nineteenth century
> during the seventies

Exception: if the century is specified for a decade, use numbers.

> during the 1970's

**h.** Form the plural of numbers by adding " 's." Quotation marks, although not required to form the plural, give emphasis to the number.

> There are three "2's" in this example.

BUT: During the seventies we prospered.

**i.** Capitalize the first half (but not the second half) of a hyphenated street name.

> Forty-second Street          Thirty-fourth Street

**j.** (1) Fractions standing alone or followed by "of a" or "of an" are spelled out and hyphenated.

> one-tenth                    one-half inch
> three-fourths of an inch     one-hundredth

(2) However, numbers are used for fractions that are part of a modifier.

$\frac{1}{2}$-mile run $\qquad\qquad$ $\frac{3}{4}$-inch pipe

(3) Numbers are used for fractions that would require more than two words.

$3\frac{1}{2}$ cartons $\qquad\qquad$ $10\frac{1}{2}$ days

(4) If the fraction is the subject and is followed by "of," the verb agrees with the noun in the phrase.

One-fourth of the pizza *was* consumed.
One-fourth of the sandwiches *were* consumed.

**k.** If a noun indicates a measurement of space, time, or money, it is singular in meaning, even if it looks plural.

Ten dollars is the price he quoted.
Thirty minutes is all the time I can give you.
Five miles is the distance from Tantown to Tooley.

**l.** Mathematical expressions can be tricky when it comes to subject-verb agreement. Use the following as patterns.

Four TIMES two ARE eight.
Four AND two ARE six.
Four PLUS two IS six.
Four MINUS two IS two.
Four DIVIDED by two IS two.
ONE-FOURTH of four IS one.

# REDUNDANCY

**240. Redundancy** refers to the use of more words than are necessary to express a meaning.

> **PAST history** (history is already past, so PAST is redundant and should be omitted)—just "history"
>
> **TRUE facts** (facts are true, so TRUE is redundant and should be omitted)—just "facts"
>
> **eliminate ALTOGETHER** (ALTOGETHER is redundant)
>
> **filled TO CAPACITY** (TO CAPACITY is redundant)
>
> **END result** (END is redundant)

In these other examples of redundancy, the capitalized words are unnecessary.

> attractive IN APPEARANCE
>
> square IN SHAPE
>
> blue IN COLOR
>
> never AT ANY TIME
>
> NEW innovation
>
> EARLY beginning (or FRESH beginning)
>
> repeat AGAIN
>
> biggest AND LARGEST
>
> MODERN car of tomorrow (or modern car OF TOMORROW)
>
> refers BACK to
>
> 3 p.m. IN THE AFTERNOON (or 3 a.m. IN THE MORNING)
>
> one SINGLE competitor
>
> may POSSIBLY be

christened AS

fewer IN NUMBER

FREE gift

YOUNG infant

surgeon BY OCCUPATION

consensus OF OPINION

biography OF HIS LIFE

last OF ALL

continue ON

FINAL settlement

MUTUAL cooperation

SERIOUS danger

UNIVERSAL panacea

**INDEX.** The numbers following the entries refer NOT to page numbers but to item numbers in the text. By matching a reference number with a guide number (top, center, of each page in the text), you can locate any item quickly.

# C

Case: possessive 35-a
  of *it* 35-c
  of noun or pronoun preceding a gerund 24-g;
    50-c
  of nouns 24, 35-a
  of pronouns 35-b, d
*Cite—sight—site* 114
Clause(s) 6
  adjective 6-e.2; 30-a
  adverb 6-e.3
  dependent 6-b; also see "Dependent Clause"
  independent 6-a; also see "Independent
    Clause"
  introduced by a colon 223-b
  main clause (same as independent clause) 6
  non-restrictive and restrictive 224-l
  noun 6-e.1
  subordinate clause (same as dependent clause)
    6
Closing of a letter: see "Complimentary
    Closing"
Collective noun
  antecedent of a pronoun 36-e
  defined 22-d
  in subject-verb agreement 47-q
Colon 223
  after salutation of a business letter 223-d
  between chapter and verse 223-e
  between hour and minute 223-e
  introduce an explanatory word, phrase, clause
    223-b
  introduce a quotation 223-c
  introduce a series 223-a
Combining sentences 21; by constructing a(an)
  appositive 21-a
  complex sentence 21-i
  compound-complex sentence 21-j
  compound object 21-g
  compound sentence 21-h
  compound subject 21-e
  compound verb 21-f
  infinitive phrase 21-c
  parallel structure 21-k
  participial phrase 21-d
  prepositional phrase 21-b
Comma(s) 224
  addresses 224-q
  appositive 19, 224-m
  avoid ambiguity 224-s
  between subject and predicate (error) 224-x
  complex sentence 11-c, 224-g
  complimentary closing of a letter 224-v
  compound sentence 11-b, 224-f
  dates and places 224-q

Comma(s) (*continued*)
  degrees and titles 224-w
  direct address 224-n
  essential (restrictive) clause or phrase 224-l
  introductory elements 224-g, h, i, o
  nonessential (non-restrictive) clause or phrase
    224-l
  omission of words 224-t
  parenthetical expressions 224-p
  quotations 224-r
  salutation of a friendly letter 224-u
  series of elements 224-a, b, c, d, e
  verbal phrase 224-i, j, k
Comma fault 14
Common gender of pronouns 36-a
Common noun 22-a, b
  used as adjective 53-a
Comparative degree
  adjectives 55-b; adverbs 62-b
*Compare to—compare with* 115
Comparison
  *as . . . as* for positive comparison; *so . . . as*
    for negative comparison 55-f, 75-e
*Complement—compliment* 116
Complements 7
  defined 7-a
  direct object 7-b; see also "Direct Object"
  indirect object 7-c
  of a linking verb 7-f
    predicate adjective
    predicate noun
    predicate pronoun
Complete subject and complete predicate 3-d
Complex sentence 11-c
  comma fault sentence corrected by a 14-d
  in sentence combining 21-i
  punctuation of 11-c
  run-on sentence corrected by a 13-d
Complimentary closing of letters 219-b, 224-v
Compound adjective 56-d, 230-a
Compound-complex sentence 11-d
  in sentence combining 21-j
Compound direct object 7-e
  case of 34-a; 34-d.1
  in sentence combining 21-g
Compound indirect object 7-e
  case of 34-b; 34-d.2
  in sentence combining 21-g
Compound noun 22-c, 23-l
  plural of a 23-l
  possessive case of a 24-e

# P

# SCORE SHEET (items 10–140)

| | |
|---|---|
| 10 | 91 |
| 11 | 92 |
| 12 | 93 |
| 13 | 94 |
| 14 | 95 |
| 15 | 96 |
| 16 | 97 |
| 20 | 98 |
| 21 | 99 |
| 23 | 100 |
| 24 | 101 |
| 27 | 102 |
| 29 | 103 |
| 30 | 104 |
| 31 | 105 |
| 33 | 106 |
| 34 | 107 |
| 35 | 108 |
| 36 | 109 |
| 37 | 110 |
| 39 | 111 |
| 40 | 112 |
| 41 | 113 |
| 45 | 114 |
| 46 | 115 |
| 47 | 116 |
| 48 | 117 |
| 49 | 118 |
| 50 | 119 |
| 55 | 120 |
| 56 | 121 |
| 62 | 122 |
| 63 | 123 |
| 69 | 124 |
| 74 | 125 |
| 75 | 126 |
| 77 | 127 |
| 78 | 128 |
| 79 | 129 |
| 80 | 130 |
| 81 | 131 |
| 82 | 132 |
| 83 | 133 |
| 84 | 134 |
| 85 | 135 |
| 86 | 136 |
| 87 | 137 |
| 88 | 138 |
| 89 | 139 |
| 90 | 140 |